Dear Ann Volume 3: Episodes 121-180

Letters to and from Teachers, Students, Parents, and More

By Ann Y. Mouse

Love Science Fiction or Mystery?

Choose your adventure!

Visit: http://www.juliecgilbert.com/

For details on getting free books.

Dedication:

To the many teachers, parents, friends, colleagues, and random strangers who answered my many questions.

To the future teachers seeking insight or advice.

To the students we serve day in and day out.

Table of Contents:

Chapter 1:
Episode 121 – Special Guest: Creative Preschool Teacher Part 1

Introduction:

Dear Reader,

One perk of teaching high schoolers is that they tend to know how to blow their noses and wash their hands. Whether they choose to do so is another matter entirely (some just sniffle every half second), but someone had to teach them the art of nose blowing.

Vital life skills like hand washing should be taught at home, but sometimes, childcare centers also have a hand in that education process.

Numbers, letters, and days on the calendar also star somewhere. I recently got to sit down and chat with a preschool teacher.

~Ann

Do you have a preference for what I call you?
No.

Me: Okay. Let's go with Creative Preschool Teacher. It's probably redundant, but it looks nice.

What age were the children you worked with? How many did you have?

Creative Pre-School Teacher: My kids were ages 2.5 to 3.5. It could vary, but generally, it was between 15 and 23 kids with one assistant.

Me: Being a curious soul, I looked up the numbers. For kids in that age range, there should be a ratio of one staff to ten students with a maximum of twenty kids. Apparently, there's a different ratio required during rest. Learn something new every day.

In any case, it's a good idea to have two staff members when dealing with kids. I always think of the complications involved in using the restroom when it comes to taking care of kids.

Why choose to teach preschool age children?

Creative Preschool Teacher: I enjoyed teaching kids. Once upon a time, I was a teacher's aide in high school. Throughout my education, I had teachers who impacted me, some good, some bad. I wanted to make a positive impact in kids' lives.

What kind of school did you work for?

Creative Preschool Teacher: I worked at a nonprofit, YMCA.

Did you have to do a demo lesson?

Creative Preschool Teacher: Yes, I read the students *The Very Hungry Caterpillar* by Eric Carle. When we got to the part that said cocoon, I replaced the word with chrysalis because that's the correct term. One of the two-year-old boys raised his hand and corrected me on what it said. I explained why I replaced it. (I got the job.)

Did you buy your own supplies or were they provided?

Creative Preschool Teacher: Some of both. They might get some of the requested supplies, but they had to make the budget stretch. Mostly, I'd buy balls for our PE time or stuff for the sensory table, books, and art supplies. Lots of art supplies.

How much money did you spend per year?

Creative Preschool Teacher: Probably $100 to $200.

What was the best thing you bought or made for your classroom?

Creative Preschool Teacher: I once made a set of alphabet cards for my students. It showed how letters are formed. A lot of the ones you can buy are in a font that adds little decorative flares that don't show the students how the letter is formed.

Did you have a prize system?

Creative Preschool Teacher: Yes, I bought sticker charts from Amazon. We'd give the students a sticker for every healthy item they ate. Since some kids didn't have healthy snacks, I would provide them for those who could not afford them.

Did you have a set curriculum to work with?

Creative Preschool Teacher: We had a list of topics we were supposed to cover, but I felt some parts of it were too young. There's only so many art projects, science projects, and other ways to teach about balls. We don't need a month for it.

Me: What kinds of things did you do to teach on the topic of balls?

Creative Preschool Teacher: The kids painted with balls. They dipped foam balls into thinned down acrylic paint. Then, they threw them at a piece of paper out in the parking lot. For a science project, the students made rubber balls.

How did you approach prep for your class?

Creative Preschool Teacher: At the beginning of the year, I broke the year down by monthly themes. Then, month to month, I'd plan out specific projects and write them into the parent newsletter that covered what we'd learn along with the developmental standards the lessons would meet.

It's a bit harder to find standards for preschool kids because they aren't on websites. We had a binder of standards that we could borrow as necessary.

What were the best and worst topics to teach?
Creative Preschool Teacher: Best topic was ...
- Music around the world – The room was decorated with different sections that celebrated different kinds of music (Flamenco dancing, Native American, Polish, Jazz and Blues, Jamaican, Irish, etc.) and the cultures that they came from. We watched videos and had pictures in each section. One of the girls painted a picture of the Flamenco dancer almost as well as an adult. That was fun to see.
- I also enjoyed the Oceans Theme.

Me: How did you set up for that one?

Creative Preschool Teacher: I turned the water sensory table into an ocean by putting sand on one side and water on the other side. The kids made jellyfish from bowls and beads on a string, so I hung these from a blue shower curtain to make it look like we were underwater.

Me: The jellyfish project sounds like fun. Kind of wish I was in your class. Beads are very soothing.

Creative Preschool Teacher: Worst topic was ...
- Numbers – It's hard to make that fun, and I hate math anyway. We did a lot of things with the calendar and the shapes of numbers. Kids made numbers out of popsicle sticks or filled in bubble numbers with colored sand.

Me: I like numbers up through multiplication and division and maybe simple algebra. After that, math and I went our separate ways.

I also happen to like numbers and counting and such, but I don't remember how I learned numbers. I remember having fun organizing the change from my mom's purse. Maybe I just like money.

That's a good stopping point.

I recently had the pleasure of watching one baby and was absolutely exhausted by the experience. I don't know how people choose to work with multiple kiddos at once.

Takeaways from part 1:
- Being a pre-school teacher requires you to bring your creativity A-game all the time.
- You can always go beyond a curriculum, like in the case of balls. If you can't fill a month with projects and experiments concerning round objects, expand.
- Taking care of kids is tough work.
- Prize systems don't have to solely revolve around behavior.

Chapter 2:
Episode 122 – Special Guest: Creative Preschool Teacher Part 2

Introduction:

Dear Reader,

Welcome back. Our current guest is still here and eager to tell us more about her adventures as a preschool teacher.

Let's talk about life skills, conflicts, and conflict resolution.

~Ann

Do you recall any odd or hostile encounters with parents?

Creative Preschool Teacher: I had one parent who was annoyed that I didn't teach his daughter multiplication and division. He even brought in a workbook for me to look at. It had work suitable for 3rd graders.

Me: How did you handle the situation?

Creative Preschool Teacher: I told him that the US doesn't consider multiplication and division age-appropriate for three-year-olds. This age is more about life skills. Then, I invited him to talk to my boss.

What life skills did you teach kids?
Creative Preschool Teacher:
- How to blow your nose
- I tried to increase their attention span.

Me: From what to what?

Creative Preschool Teacher: From about 10 minutes to 30 minutes.

I wanted them to be able to sit through Circle Time, which consisted of a song, a story, weather information, and a small calendar lesson.

- Numbers. We counted up to the 100th day of school then had a 100-day party. After that, we counted by 10's.
- How to wash your hands properly.

Me: That sounds difficult. How did you do that?

Creative Preschool Teacher:
- I got some glitter glue to simulate germs. The kids lathered up with it, then they got soap and washed it off. Most still had glitter on them.
- Next, I did the same. I put some glitter glue on myself and lathered up with it. Then, I demonstrated proper washing techniques while singing the ABCs.
- The kids tried again. This time, we worked to a modified version of the Baby Bumblebee song.

Me: That's brilliant. I've still outlawed glitter in my classroom, but it is a good use of glitter glue. (And now I have Baby Bumblebee in my head, thanks.)

What brought you out of teaching?
Creative Preschool Teacher: Politics.

- It got more difficult to teach because we ended up dealing with culture of nothing is wrong. We could not discipline the kids at all. There was/is an errant thought that even time out could scar the kids. As a result, students got violent. They would scratch and hit without consequences. Maybe it was pandering to parents, I don't know, but regardless, time outs were no longer allowed.

- They also wanted to extend the age range of my class from 2 to 3.5. It may not seem like much, but six months is a long time at that age. The children are at completely different developmental stages.

- It was suggested that I just run two circle times. That would have been chaos. Teaching 1st through 3rd grade would be hard but doable, but 2 to 3.5 is much harder because the kids' attention span is simply not there.

- My boss was a business major not an expert in education. The CEO wanted the center to make more money. So, even though people were telling her the best ways to run things for the kids' sake, she was listening to her boss and making decisions accordingly.

- The state was stepping in more. If I had continued on, I would have been asked to teach things I don't think are appropriate for children that age.

- It's important to teach kids life lessons when they are very young, and the organization was making that difficult.

What are the most important lessons for young children to learn?
Creative Preschool Teacher:
- How to solve people problems

- How to communicate – screaming because you're angry doesn't solve things

How did you handle discipline if you couldn't use time out?

Creative Preschool Teacher: I replaced time out with a Think About it Spot. If someone was angry, they could go there to think about what's wrong, find the words to convey what is wrong, and then, come tell a teacher.

My father taught me that whenever I'm angry, I should write it out, sleep on it, then revisit the issue the next day.

Me: I never really thought about how difficult it must be to express feelings without an extensive vocabulary.

Two stories about discipline matters:

Creative Preschool Teacher: Story One: I had a three-year-old with anger issues. More specifically, he had a difficult time verbalizing anger. He once said, "I hate you!"

Me: How did you respond to that?

Creative Preschool Teacher: I told him I'm sorry u feel that way. "I love you. And that's not going to change." That answer seemed to startle him because nobody had ever said something like that to him.

Story Two: I had one girl who never wanted to clean up her toys. She declared that she wasn't going to do it. So, I said, "Okay, if you don't want to act like a big kid, I will help you like I would help a little kid."

I then took her hand and put the toys away using her hand. Eventually, she pulled her hand away, said she was a big kid, and proceeded to put the toys away herself.

What skills are helpful to have when entering a job like this?
Creative Preschool Teacher:
- Creativity
- Patience
- Good people skills – You will need to handle parents, kids, colleagues, and bosses.
- Communication skills – You will be teaching kids communication skills, so it helps to have them as well.
- Organization skills
- A good sense of timing and knowing how long things should take. – Kids have short attention spans, so you need to mix things up.

Did you enjoy being a teacher? What did you enjoy about it?
Creative Preschool Teacher: At the beginning, I enjoyed teaching.
- The kids were fun.
- I enjoyed opening their eyes to the world and helping them be better humans.
- I even got to talk to them about God if they brought it up.

Takeaways:
- Politics (and too much meddling in general by people disconnected from actual teaching) has the potential to make things very difficult.
- Patience is vital for teaching young children.

Communication skills are helpful no matter what you do in life.

Chapter 3:
Episode 123 – Special Guest: Concerns of an Exhausted Teacher Returning to School

Introduction:

Dear Reader,

Our next guest chose to avail herself of the google form instead of doing an interview. Honestly, I love both the interviews and the forms because it lets people tell their story in a way that's comfortable for them.

She shares some of her concerns about returning to school. From our brief conversations about the topic, it's more than just a return after summer break. I gather that she took a year-long break from teaching but is returning to the same district she taught at before.

Some background: She's worn many different stakeholder hats. She's a parent, former teacher, soon-to-be current teacher, community member, and a past schoolboard member.

Every situation is unique, and each of those stakeholders has slightly different points of view.

~Ann

Dear Ann,

I'm starting teaching over. (I'll probably fill out this form a few times.)

Why do districts keep their curriculum and yearly topic schedules locked away so you need permission to view it?

(I understand no edits, but views?! I've been frustrated by this as a parent in that I couldn't look ahead to entice—or come up with incentives to suffer through with my children.

But also, as a new educator in a district—2nd time now—it's impossible to see any details without a district email, and difficult with it.

Why do districts hold it so close to the cuff?

It would be easy enough to include disclaimers that individual school/teacher discretion may be applied as to the exact timing, blah, blah, blah.

As an aside, I do my onboarding paperwork tomorrow (which should be minor since I already work in the district), and I'm having a mild panic attack about returning to the bureaucracy and crappiness in two weeks.

It's a solid team and good school in a good district, but I have concerns outweighing excitement. Access to curriculum would really help alleviate that ... thanks for reading!

~ Exhausted Teacher

Dear Exhausted Teacher,

Thanks for sharing. I hope you have a very smooth transition back, but I would also enjoy hearing the good, the bad, and the ugly that goes along with your new teaching saga.

Congrats on the invite back to teach. I hope the time off gave you time to recharge.

I'm a little concerned that you're calling yourself Exhausted Teacher two weeks before the year starts, though I do vividly recall that can be a very busy time of year.

Much of the country is returning to school from the summer, so you're at least in good company about feeling anxiety about kicking off a new school year.

To your question, one thing school districts—and to be fair, everybody—does best is cover their butts.

I believe your difficulty in getting access to the curriculum is part of this blanket policy. You might choose to use knowledge of the curriculum to motivate your children, but I can see that going awry in the hands of other parents.

Why?
Because people complain about everything. If the curriculum was easily accessible by all, most would ignore it, but some would check it out. A few would read it with the specific aim to find some fault with it.

Are there faults with any curriculum?
Absolutely.

Should they be addressed?
Yes.

By whom?
By whoever needs to teach the curriculum in the coming year. Some stuff is mandated by the state, and some is just set in place by whatever company had the original product that got modified.

Some schools just had a teacher share what they did and so on down the line, but most have some form of online curriculum now.

Aside: This brings up a wider issue of Us vs. Them, which I've often found sad because parents and teachers want what's best for kids. The conflicts kick in when there's a difference in the definition of what is best for kids.

Change it where you can:

All that said, I write weekly newsletters to let people know what's going on in my classes. It's a system that works for me. You're right in saying that there isn't much openness about what's ahead in each class, especially as the students get older.

If that system works for you, go for it. If it doesn't, find your own way to keep people in the loop.

Back on track:

You bring up some excellent points about technological access. I've heard of it taking two weeks for the technology department to get around to creating district emails for new teachers.

In theory, it should be an easy thing, but small things like that get lost in the shuffle.

You also mentioned bureaucracy. (I absolutely hate spelling that word too. It's like the word itself needlessly involves more letters than necessary just to befuddle people.)

In this case, we're working with one of the sub definitions, the one that deals with red tape.

Unless you have a separate in with a tech person, you're not likely to get a swift response because the message has to trickle through a few people.

Hopefully, you can contact the right people to get bumped up the priority list because knowledge would certainly help you prepare, which would indeed ease some nerves.

Paperwork:

Paperwork is the less exciting part of any job, but since that's how you get paid, get insurance, and so forth, I guess it's a necessary evil.

Dealing with back-to-school jitters:

Some of the advice applies to all teachers. Some is specific to your situation. Take what you need. Disregard the rest.

- You have done this before.
- Every year is a unique challenge.
- Enjoy the parts you can.
- Set up a good support system for the frustrating parts.

These can vary, though I recommend not social media. (A private journal, a trusted confidant, a ritualistic Friday night ice cream special to de-stress, a few audiobooks about serial killers, etc. ... whatever works for you.)

- Find a system that works for you for everything: planning, breaking away to spend time with family, grading, morning routine, board setup.
- Establish your kingdom and show the kids if you love what you do.
- Communicate well in a way that's comfortable for you. If emails are your thing, email away. If you love Post-it notes, leave peppy ones around your room. If you love stuffed animals, fill your room with them. If you have a particularly ornery chicken you want to show off, have a framed portrait on your desk. (To some extent) it doesn't matter what the cool thing is, just make the space yours.

Takeaways:
- Schools aren't very open about their curriculums.
- Communication as a teacher is important.
- Prepare as best you can. Try not to worry about the rest. (Or find good coping mechanisms to weather the stress.)

Chapter 4:
Episode 124 – Special Guest:
Passionate Adolescent Therapist
Part 1 – Background

Introduction:
Dear Reader,

Finding anybody to talk to me about their experiences related to school can be difficult. I believe a lot of people doubt their ability to add something new to the conversation.

Teachers, former teachers, and parents tend to be a smidge easier to convince I come in peace.

That makes it an extra special treat to welcome our current guest. She is a parent, but today, she's talking to us as a therapist who works in a school.

~Ann

What would you like me to call you?
Adolescent Therapist

Me: As I read through your answers, the word passionate came to mind, so I'm going to add that and call you Passionate Adolescent Therapist. That's short for Passionate Adolescent Therapist Who Works in a Middle School.

Did you have friends in high school?

Passionate Adolescent Therapist: I did. I was very involved in clubs/activities, so I had a lot of acquaintances. I also always had a small close group of true friends. My current *best friends* are actually two women who I became friends with in 4th grade.

Me: It's great that you kept in touch with those friends through the years.

Did you get close to any teachers when you were a student?

Passionate Adolescent Therapist: My 4th grade teacher, Mrs. J., was amazing. I had her at a time when I didn't believe in myself. (Long story short: I wasn't chosen for enrichment that year while all my friends were.)

Mrs. J. helped me to believe in myself. I had a lot of social anxiety, and she helped to make me feel safe and loved.

My 8th grade Math teacher, Mrs. M., was so sweet and kind to me. She was also a fantastic math teacher. When I had a not-so-great teacher in the 9th grade, Mrs. M. always made herself available to me for extra help.

I came to know my AP Biology teacher, S., more in a friendly way, outside of class. He was a remarkable biology teacher but was all business in the classroom. I got to know him well, as my family and I would always volunteer to help him with the annual scholarship run.

Coincidentally, I ended up at the same gym as him during my senior year, and he would always come talk to me and was really encouraging about the progress I was making.

Me: Your experiences highlight the fact that there are multiple ways to connect with students. Unifying themes here are kindness, support, and sharing common interests.

How many years have you worked in a school?
Passionate Adolescent Therapist: I'm going into my tenth year of running the in-school clinical program.

I also have been working for a psychiatrist in private practice for six years.

Did you have a different career or was social work your first career?
Passionate Adolescent Therapist: I graduated from NYU with my Master of Social Work Degree in 2006.

- My first job was in an adult inpatient psychiatric hospital.
- I then worked at a Therapeutic public high school, but I was RIF'd (Reduction in Force – terminated because of restructuring, changing of departments, etc.) after one year. It was my absolute dream job, and I was heartbroken.
- I then worked at an outpatient substance abuse clinic which was horrible, and then at a high level of care (partial-hospital and intensive outpatient treatment) clinic with adolescents.

Me: *runs to Google to figure out what the heck RIF stands for.* Turns out, it stands for Reduction in Force. I'd only ever heard the term layoff, and apparently, that's got a different meaning.

Side note: Every time I think of this kind of thing, I think of Emperor Kuzco's speech. ("You're being let go, your department's being downsized, you're part of an outplacement...")

Second side note: Teachers tend to be non-renewed before tenure since the teaching contracts go year to year.

Sorry, let's get back on track.

Why did you choose social work?
Passionate Adolescent Therapist:
- I was always fascinated by all things social worker-y.
- I actually found a paper I wrote in middle school about how I wanted to become a psychiatric social worker.
- I love working with people, and I'm never bored (quite the opposite).

Why work in a school?
Passionate Adolescent Therapist:
- Honestly, if I said that I didn't gravitate towards working in a school for the hours, I'd be lying. That was/is a big piece.
- I also feel like I'm able to help students and families to make progress and to grow emotionally, during some of the most formative years of their life.
- In the school, I'm not restricted by insurance or any type of crap that dictates how long I can work with someone.
- I'm able to work with a student as long as they need. I have many of the students for the entirety of their time in middle school.

What kind of school do you work in?
Passionate Adolescent Therapist: I work for a company that has a contract for me to provide services in the district where I am. I am contracted to be in a public middle school.

How long does it take you to prepare to do your job in a typical week?
Passionate Adolescent Therapist:
I run three different types of groups a week:
- Process Group (talking) – All I need to do for process group is to set up the room.

- Psychoeducational Group (learning) – I have to pick an activity or develop a lesson that supports the topic for the month. This could take anywhere from ten minutes to an hour depending on how focused I am. It's faster if I'm reusing a lesson.
- Feedback Group (which is reviewing teacher's feedback, part of the reward system used). – Feedback group takes the longest to prepare for, as I have to reach out to teachers (usually multiple times) asking for the weekly feedback. I then have to review it and tally points for each form I receive for the student and then identify their 'score' for the week (which is the average).
- I usually have two different cohorts of students, so I run two process groups, two psychoeducational groups, and then one feedback group a week.
- I do a combined feedback group because it is often more impactful to run this as a bigger group.

What was your favorite topic or program to teach?

Passionate Adolescent Therapist: My favorite topics I cover in psycho-ed groups are coping skills and Cognitive Behavioral Therapy.

I also like to teach about gratitude.

What was your least favorite topic or program to teach?

Passionate Adolescent Therapist: I don't like when it is the month to focus on family of origin. With older kids this is a great topic, but I find with middle schoolers it often makes them mad, feel more helpless/hopeless, and/or the concept of family shaping behavior goes right over their heads.

Me: This is a good stopping point. Next round, we'll dig more into more impressions of the job and advice.

Takeaways:
- School hours can be an awesome perk.
- Some people know what they want to do right away.
- Support and kindness, especially from a teacher, can go a long way in making a kid feel safe.
- Being a therapist rarely leads to boredom.
- It's also very rewarding to work with kids during their formative years.

Chapter 5:
Episode 125 – Special Guest:
Passionate Adolescent Therapist
Part 2 – Ups, Downs, and Advice

Introduction:
Dear Reader,

Being a therapist does not sound easy.

Every job has tough stuff, but this job deals specifically with hard things kids deal with.

I only know the feedback forms from the other side, the teaching side. I can see why those would be averages. It was intriguing to hear how they're used.

Today, Passionate Adolescent Therapist will explore the high and low points of her job before leaving us with some sage advice.

~Ann

What is the best, worst, and most fun part of your job?

Passionate Adolescent Therapist:

Best part of the job:

- The best part of my job is when I see adolescents and/or their family making changes and improving their mental health, or when someone I work with writes me a heartfelt note acknowledging their progress.
- I also love when I have an adolescent or young adult come back to see me and let me know everything is okay (that they have a job, or they are going to college).

Me: It is always intriguing to hear from past students or see what they're up to on social media.

Worst part of the job:

- The worst part is suicide attempts, hands-down.
- Significant self-injury is also so hard. It is absolutely heartbreaking to see that someone is so desperate for relief that they hurt themselves.
- The other worst part involves my LGBTQIA kiddos. I have so many students who identify on different areas of the spectrum of sexuality and/or gender.
- It's so hard to see these students rejected by their families or have their experiences minimized, especially with all of the research that shows what rejection does to the LGBTQIA person's mental health and will to live.
- It's hard to get the teachers to understand the importance of using correct pronouns and how it can minimize the risk of suicide by 40% to just call someone what they prefer to be called.

Most fun part of the job:

- The most fun part of my job is when I see my students acting like kids.
- When they are being silly or getting along or having fun ... those moments are priceless.
- The other most fun part of my job is when my group just clicks, and suddenly this motley crew of middle schoolers becomes a family!

Do you have any advice for new therapists?
Passionate Adolescent Therapist:

- I'd tell a new therapist to talk less and listen more.
- I'd tell them what a gift it is to have someone trust you with their story, especially when that is the only thing that person has.
- I'd tell them to treat everyone with dignity and respect, and to come from the perspective that everyone is doing the best they can with what they have. If they could do better, they would.
- I'd also remind them that much of the research about the efficacy of the different types of therapy says it doesn't actually matter. That the relationship a person has with their therapist is the greatest indicator of success and improvement.

What do you think kids need to succeed at school?
Passionate Adolescent Therapist:

- Kids need to be safe and secure.
- They need to feel that the adults they are interacting with really give a crap about them and are happy they are there.
- They need the ability to be who they are without fear of rejection.
- They need to have their basic needs met both inside and outside of school.

- They also need more sleep, less internet usage, and access to mental health services.

Me: That's quite the list. Some of those points seem obvious, but then again, sometimes, we need to see the straightforward points listed out in an easy-to-digest list.

How did the pandemic affect teaching and therapy?
Passionate Adolescent Therapist:
I saw a lot of teachers phone it in, but I also saw a large number of teachers busting their butts to meet the needs of their students.

In terms of therapy, the pandemic was both a blessing and a curse. I think the increase in accessibility and affordability of teletherapy has been a miracle for so many people, especially those who don't live in areas where they can easily access services.

The downside is that business is booming, and with the increase in demand comes horrible therapists who are in it to make money.

Me: Money is tricky. It's necessary in the society we live in, but the obsession with it has the potential to ruin much.

If you were given an unlimited budget and a year to make any changes to education systems/ your school, what changes would you make?
- I'd create a system that wraps the school up in community supports and services.
- Where kids receive free breakfast, lunch, and transportation daily.
- I'd make uniforms mandatory, with funding for those who can't afford it, to get rid of the obvious disparity between the rich and low-income students who attend school.
- Every student and their family would have access to comprehensive medical care and treatment on a sliding scale.

- There would be more education about resilience and coping skills, problem solving and conflict resolution instead of this push for mindfulness (which has truly become twisted).
- The school would provide parent education classes, using evidence-based programs at times that working parents could attend, and a caseworker who would meet with families to identify their needs and help them to get those needs met.
- Since I'd have an unlimited budget, I'd strive to create a community like the Harlem Children's Zone!

Me: *Once again Googling.*

From my brief exploration, it looks like the overarching Harlem Children's zone program is designed to hit many of the points in Passionate Adolescent Therapist's ideal education system.

In short, it seeks to support families in and out of schools through many programs that go beyond classrooms. (aid, health and wellness, academic support, etc.)

The uniform comment surprised me. It seems like such a small point. Kids would find a way to show their status, but I agree it would make the money thing less obvious.

Takeaways:
- Relationships matter in teaching and in therapy.
- Rejection is devastating. Small gestures can go a long way in helping a kid feel accepted.
- Kids need to be safe and secure first. Academic education takes place after that.
- The pandemic was a make-or-break point for many teachers. But one good thing to come of it was an increase in access to teletherapy.

Chapter 6:
Episode 126 – A Very Short Interview and the I-Would-Nevers

Introduction:

Dear Reader,

This next guest is one of my former students. Once again, this ranks among the things that make teachers feel very old.

It's not quite as sobering as teaching the children of former students, but it's right up there with seeing former students get married and have babies.

Some people have a lot to say, and others keep their answers short and sweet. Since Vellas have a word count requirement, I thought I'd also share more stuff I dug up from social media.

~Ann

Since she didn't answer the question about what she wanted me to call her, I shall go with Former Student, which is short for Former Student Who Became a Teacher and Now Left Teaching and is Making Me Feel Old.

Chapter Part 1: Short Interview
How many years did you teach?
Former Student: 4

What is the best, worst, and most fun part of teaching?
Former Student:
- The best part is seeing the growth your students make and their love for learning.
- The worst part is getting blamed for things I have no control over especially during the pandemic.
- The most fun part is just being able to be myself with my students and be silly.

Me: Ah. If I'm calculating this correctly, this guest did one, maybe two, years of teaching before the pandemic exploded onto the scene and rearranged the landscape.

I can see how that would turn anybody off from the profession, but I'm also sure it wasn't just one reason. People come to and leave the teaching profession for many reasons.

Side note: I would add that one of the best parts of teaching hearing from former students. Even if what they choose to do has nothing to do with your class, it's intriguing to see where they end up in life.

Do you have any advice for new teachers?
- Set clear boundaries between work and life.
- It is too easy to burn out quickly.
- If you don't care for yourself, you can't take care of your students.

Me: This is good advice regardless of profession. I just think it's talked about more in relation to teaching.

Now that you're done with teaching, what will you do?

Former Student: I'm doing business development at J.P. Morgan!

***

Chapter Part 2: The I-Would-Nevers ...

One person's answer:

- Unless answer is get paid an appropriate salary – yeah you would

Me: I found this statement amusing. Salary comes up a lot usually in a negative context. Starting salaries are all over the place. Public school teacher salaries are a matter of public record, so if you're inclined, you could look up a particular school and see what their current pay scale is.

Many teachers do have a side hustle of some sort. Sometimes, it's a necessity, but sometimes, it's a choice. Since teaching pays the bills and writing money does not, I'd consider writing a side hustle. Enter the profession with an idea of what you need to get by. If teaching doesn't cut it, get a job that will support you and your family.

The actual I-would-nevers ...

- Treat aides, bus drivers, cooks, etc. as less than myself
- Fall asleep with a class

Me: I take naps at school, but they're on my periods off. My kids don't get organized nap time anyway, so this isn't an issue for me in that regard.

Never say never:

- Go to duty. Just say no.

Me: I don't consider this great advice, but I can see frustration building to an unhealthy point. If you need to miss a duty, you can usually get permission to skip out, but they are a part of the job you signed up for. If you're untenured, definitely don't listen to that advice.

- Make it to the end of the day.

Me: There will be days where it feels that way, but you'll make it. You might not have much left in the energy reserves, but you'll make it.

The things we say "I would never" until we do.
- Yell at kids
- Curse a kid out

Me: There's always a fine line. Kids do need expectations and discipline. Much as we like the idea of complete freedom that translates to anarchy which is not productive.

Nobody should be cursing anybody out.

To be fair, there are likely times the kid 100% deserves to be taken down a few dozen notches, but cursing doesn't help. Some kids think its funny to make the teacher lose their cool. They're also often immature or putting on obnoxious airs to get attention.

Do everything in your power to remain calm.

If the situation gets to a point where it negatively affects your mental health, re-evaluate the situation. Is it the right job for you? There is nothing wrong with deciding, you're not meant to do this anymore.

- Become an admin

Me: This one is absolutely true. Nope. Not seeking certification. Not even looking into remote possibilities. It's not happening.

- Eat in front of kids

Me: I try not to, setting a good example and all, but sometimes, they want help when I'm eating breakfast. In those cases, congratulations, you get to watch me eat.

- Allow kids to do ...

Me: I try to make it clear to my students that I have a set amount of things to accomplish in a day. If they can work through those things in a reasonable time, any extra time is their to handle as they wish. (That means phone time.)

- Use inferior crayons
- Spend my own money

Me: I've never personally said any of those, especially the last one. Spending my money on school supplies never bothered me. I think it's because I just considered it equipment to do my job. And I'm picky about my pens.

- Let a kid sleep in class

Me: It depends on the situation, but generally, kids who can't stay awake are sent to the nurse.

- Have favorite students

Me: Favorites are inevitable. The important part is to attempt to treat every student as if they were/are your favorite student, even if they annoy the crap out of you.

- Chew gum while teaching
- Let a kid use a phone in class
- Teach in (fill-in-the-blank) state
- Compare students to older siblings
- Refuse to give food to a hungry kid

Me: I keep snacks. Only a few kids have been bold enough to ask for anything. If we're in class, they're definitely getting a *Nope*. Otherwise, depends on the moment.

- Spend so much on Teachers Pay Teachers

Me: I've never bought anything from there, but I can see it being an excellent starting point. I'm just very particular with how I format my worksheets, notes, presentations, and such.

- Change a grade to avoid a parent interaction
- Just give a worksheet (gets covid, two weeks of worksheets)

Me: Life happens. To the best of your abilities, plan for that fact.

Takeaways:
- Some people teach for many years. Some teach for a few years. There's no right or wrong in either path.
- There will always be kids who need good teachers and people who step up to be teachers for a time.
- It's easy to say I would never to a lot of things, but compromise in certain situations can be good for maintaining peace. That could be order in the classroom or peace of mind.

Chapter 7:
Episode 127 – Special Guest: Master Math Teacher

Introduction:

Dear Reader,

Everything has a circle of life.

The last Chapter featured a super short interview with one of my former students. So, it's fitting that this Chapter stars one of my former teachers.

I believe this man taught me Algebra, Geometry, and Advanced Algebra/Trig. (I went to a small private school, so I'm pretty sure he was <u>the</u> math teacher.)

It's not his fault I don't get along with math beyond basic algebra. From what I remember, he tried his best to make math fun and practical.

~Ann

What would you like me to call you?

Masterful Math Teacher

Me: You got it.

Did you get close to any teachers when you were a student?

Masterful Math Teacher: I went to a small private school, so I was pretty close with most of my teachers. My Phys Ed teacher was like a second father to me.

Did you have friends in high school?

Masterful Math Teacher: I was pretty popular I suppose. President of the class, President of the Choir, in the drama club, played 3 sports. Yeah, I had lots of friends.

How many years have you been teaching?

Masterful Math Teacher: I've been teaching since 1995 so 27 years.

Me: Wow. That's great. Also, slightly intimidating. I realize I must have been fairly early in your teaching career.

Did you have a different career before becoming a teacher?

Masterful Math Teacher: Started school for architectural engineering, then realized teaching and young people were my passions.

Why did you choose teaching?

Masterful Math Teacher: I realized that I wanted to influence young people.

I worked with young people every summer in high school, and after my father passed away in my freshman year of college, I realized I didn't want to waste my youth in some stuffy business. In my Junior year, I added secondary education as a major.

Was teaching your first career?

Masterful Math Teacher: Yup ... It's all I have ever done (outside of a slew of varying summer jobs).

Me: I love that there is no right or wrong path. Some people have careers that take them into and out of teaching many times, and some people jump in and stay for the long haul.

How long does it take you to prep for your classes?

Masterful Math Teacher: Hmm, tough question.

Prepping was never too hard for me, but I always spent a ton of hours trying to make things easy and enjoyable for the kids (and for me).

How do you approach prep?

Masterful Math Teacher: Truthfully, I just kind of think of how I can communicate a subject that so many people find challenging. It always starts with: how can I get students to connect with what I am trying to teach in a way that they feel is meaningful?

Me: True. Math does have a reputation to conquer.

What kind of school did/do you work in?

Masterful Math Teacher: Started in a private high school, and then, made the jump to the public sector.

Spent my first 21 years teaching high school, and then, decided it was time for a change and took on middle school.

Me: The world certainly needs great middle school teachers.

What classes did/do you teach?

Masterful Math Teacher: I have taught it all when it comes to math: General Math, Algebra I, Algebra II, PreCalculus, Calculus Honors, Calc AB and BC, Probability and Statistics.

The only class that I have taught EVERY single year is

GEOMETRY.

What was the most preps you had in a year?
Masterful Math Teacher: 3

What is your favorite class to teach?
Masterful Math Teacher: I loved teaching PreCalculus and Calculus. Have grown to really like Geometry as well.

Me: I don't think I met Calculus until college. We were not friends, but it was required for my major.

What is your favorite topic to teach?
Masterful Math Teacher: Trigonometry (Precalc) and Circles (Geometry)

What was your least favorite class to teach?
Masterful Math Teacher: Algebra II

What is the best, worst, and most fun part of teaching?
Masterful Math Teacher:
- The best part is the relationships you make with the students and other teachers.
- The worst part is the lesson plans.
- The most fun ... making students laugh.

Do you have any advice for new teachers?
Masterful Math Teacher:
- Love what you do.
- It is a job, but you also need to enjoy it to make it in this field.
- Don't take yourself too seriously.
- Always think of new, creative ways to engage the students.

What do you think kids need to succeed at school?
Masterful Math Teacher: A will to learn, and a teacher that is willing to help them flourish.

Are you involved in any extracurriculars as a teacher?
Masterful Math Teacher: Yes, I coach baseball and soccer.

When do you think the emphasis on grades kicks in?
Masterful Math Teacher:
- For students ... I think around sophomore year.
- For parents ... probably 6th or 7th grade. Parents often put a lot of pressure on the children.

How did the pandemic affect teaching?
Masterful Math Teacher:
The pandemic was a really trying time to be a teacher.

Virtual teaching with no cameras on and students often not paying attention was incredibly challenging.

We are still suffering the effects of the pandemic in the educational arena.
- Students still are adjusting to school and making relationships with other students.
- Students are struggling with balancing their social lives and academic lives.

While we have made some strides, there is still a long way to go to get students to a place where they are thriving in this new educational setting.

The good news is that we went through the most difficult time and found out new ways to incorporate technology that can help us refocus/reimagine how we teach.

This is a hard but exciting time as we try to figure out how to engage students in today's world.

How many more years do you expect to teach?

Masterful Math Teacher: Well, I'm taking classes for my principal and administrative cert currently. Might be transitioning to Dean this year, so who knows. If I get the dean position, this could be the end of my teaching years.

Me: Yes, but you'll still be in education. I hope it works out well for you.

Takeaways:

- You can change jobs within the teaching profession. Private schools are different arenas than public schools. The same goes for middle vs. high school.
- No matter what you do, love it or leave it.
- Creativity is one of the pillars of reaching and engaging students.
- The pandemic was a difficult time in education, but it forced some advances in technology integration into classrooms.

Chapter 8:
Episode 128 – Special Guest: Retired Industrial Arts Teacher
Part 1 - Background

Introduction:

Dear Reader,

Last Chapter featured a long-haul teacher who started his career teaching and hasn't stopped since.

Today, we get to visit with someone with a very different perspective. He's held several jobs, including sales positions for huge corporations, but the beginning and end of his working life are marked by teaching jobs.

This is also the first time I've gotten a shop teacher to talk to me. The interview was also done live over zoom, which allows for a more dynamic flow of questions.

I can tell this is going to go into multiple Chapters, and I can say for certain that I learned from the interview. I hope you enjoy his answers as much as I did.

~Ann

What would you like me to call you?

Nick, Recently Retired Industrial Arts Teacher

Me: I'm going to abbreviate that some. Let's go with RR Industrial Arts Teacher.

How many years did you teach?

RR Industrial Arts Teacher: Overall, I taught about 15 years, though that was broken up over several positions and different times.

Teaching Round One:
Please tell us about that journey.

RR Industrial Arts Teacher: The first 5 years after college, I taught in an Alternative education school. The students were high school aged, but academically, they didn't progress much past elementary school due to a variety of reasons.

Most weren't successful at anything. There were problems at home. I had to get good at fostering success in them despite the obstacles.

I stopped that for two main reasons:
1. Burnout
2. Finances – There just wasn't enough money in it.

What did you do next?

RR Industrial Arts Teacher: I had my own cabinet-making business for over a year. Then, another teaching opportunity came up, and I took it.

Teaching Round Two:
What was the new teaching position like?
RR Industrial Arts Teacher: Messy.

The teacher before me basically destroyed the program. He had his favorite students—the ones with the most talent for the work—creating sections of deck. Then, on the weekends, he'd install them for people who bought them from him. The rest of the kids who were not working on deck sections could do whatever they wanted. That made the class sort of a wreck.

That sounds like a really rough way to start. What did you do?

RR Industrial Arts Teacher: For starters, I fixed the place (the shop).

There were no tools, so I stocked the shop with my tools. I had promises from administration that I could buy new things when the next budget time rolled around.

Due to the lack of discipline beforehand, the kids were especially hard to manage. They were used to mayhem. The first few months were difficult.

When I put in for a budget, the Vice Principal essentially laughed and said no way to spending money on the program.

I realized then that they didn't really want a teacher, they wanted a babysitter. Since they didn't care about the program's success, I left for a job in machinery sales that paid 2-3 times what the teaching salary was at the time.

The salary alone would be reason enough, but it sounds like you had plenty of other reasons to leave that second teaching position. What was your sales job like?

RR Industrial Arts Teacher: It was for a big company, good money, and taught me a lot about business and machinery.

I was used to working with small machines, but this was industrial size equipment.

Mini-history aside that's relevant:

After World War II, Europe was a mess. (Land was destroyed, many people were dead, etc.) Out of necessity, Europeans made some radical changes to how cabinets were made. It was very methodical and used cheap materials. They accomplished this by using very efficient equipment.

So, (hypothetical example) you went from needing 50 people to make 3 kitchens a week to being able to have 10 people make 25 kitchens in a week.

There was a tech boom in the industry because American companies had to adapt or get crushed by European competition.

That sounds typical for progress. What did you get out of this new job?

RR Industrial Arts Teacher:

- I got to see a lot of historical machinery.
- I made great contacts in the industry.
- I also got a huge education in every aspect of the arts— equipment and business side.

It was a family-owned business. The father was a genius. His father owned a small business, but this man took that business and expanded it.

What did that company specialize in?

RR Industrial Arts Teacher: The company dealt with machine repair technology. We sold woodworking machines.

- I traveled more. Went to trade shows and such.
- I learned more.
- Since the company only had about 25 salesmen, each one had a big territory.
- My territory was smaller than some but densely packed.

How long did you work there?

RR Industrial Arts Teacher: 15 years.

What happened?
RR Industrial Arts Teacher: Upper management happened.
They messed up so badly that they had to sell the company.
I lost respect for corporate governing entities.

When I'd first gotten to the company, the secretaries knew more about that business and how it worked than most people walking around.

After corporate blunders, the company got bought out. This happened several times by bigger and bigger companies. Each time, they'd add more things for us to sell.

Was that why you left?
RR Industrial Arts Teacher: Yes and no.

The company had an unwritten rule that they would try to push you out after 55. They liked hiring kids right out of college because they didn't have to pay them as much. True, but the kid fresh from college also doesn't understand the business. People who have been with a business for years know it inside and out.

Things a kid fresh from college won't know about sales:
- The technical knowledge of the product. There's only so much you can learn from a book or manual.
- Taking responsibility
- Asking customers to take financial risks
- Developing relationships with customers
- Helping customers
- Gaining customer trust

They offered me an early retirement package. At first, I said no because I wanted to keep working, but somebody off-the-record warned me that if I didn't take the deal, the company would be looking for ways to get rid of me.

So, I took the deal.

Yikes, that sounds like a rough deal.
RR Industrial Arts Teacher: It's also illegal, but the chances of winning a lawsuit against a billion-dollar company are low.

That experience left me frustrated with sales, but I remembered my experiences at the alternative school. It got me thinking about teaching again.

Me: Excellent. I definitely want to hear about that, but it's time to wrap this Chapter up.

Takeaways:

- Every teaching experience is different.
- Alternative schools have a high turnover in staff due to burnout.
- Teaching can be a rewarding career, but it's not exactly a get-rich-quick thing.

Chapter 9:
Episode 129 – Special Guest: Recently Retired Industrial Arts Teacher Part 2 – Teaching Round Three and Covid

Introduction:

Dear Reader,

In the last Chapter, we heard about Recently Retired Industrial Arts Teacher's first two teaching experiences and other jobs that gave him life experience and taught him more about the other side of machines.

Today, we've reached his third teaching job.

~Ann

Mini-Recap:

When unofficially forced into early retirement, our guest remembered his teaching experiences at the alternative school.

Specifically, he remembered that he'd made a difference in kids' lives. They'd come back years later and tell him that they remembered that class.

The alternative school had a small teacher to student ratio, so he got to work closely with kids and give them more individualized instruction.

Me: The alt school job wasn't all fun, games, and memorable triumphs, but the passage of time has a way of distancing us from the horrors and trials of specific teaching moments.

Before we jump into the third teaching experience, please share a memorable moment from any of your teaching days.

RR Industrial Arts Teacher: One of the kids at my first school set his desk on fire.

Me: Yup, that qualifies.

Tell us about getting your third teaching job.

RR Industrial Arts Teacher: I didn't really want to retire, and I still had bills.

There still wasn't much money in teaching, but I was open to the idea of it again. A local suburban district had a job opening, so I applied and received the offer.

Even in good school systems, there can be bad teachers. My predecessor at the third school was fired. (He was mentally abusive to the students.)

Whether they were just desperate or believed I would do a good job, they needed a body in the room, so I got it even though I hadn't taught in quite a few years.

Me: I haven't had that long of a break between teaching jobs, but I've had a few different ones and can confirm that every position is vastly different anyway.

What did you do when you got to your new school?
RR Industrial Arts Teacher: I had a lot of work to do before the school year opened.

The equipment was junky, in poor repair, and very poorly organized. The shop was essentially set up for failure.

- I needed most of that first year to put things in order and get the equipment to a usable point.
- I also had to change the class culture very quickly. Due to my predecessor's handling, the kids had gotten used to looking for easy grades.
- Pushed for new equipment, and my boss understood the value in it. Furthermore, he put in the effort to get me the equipment I asked for.

It was a lot of work, but at least it paid off. The program's been decent since the changes I implemented.

What did you ask for?
RR Industrial Arts Teacher: I wanted a CNC machine for the class because I wanted to teach a separate course on that.

Me: *Types that down furiously, knowing I'll be searching that up later. I ended up asking our guest what it stood for, and he was kind enough to explain.

RR Industrial Arts Teacher: CNC stands for Computer Numeric Control. It tells the machine how far to move, how fast to move, and where to move. It's robotics and production combined.

It's a coordinate system. (Usually x, y, z.) The computer changes the coordinates to code. The software can fashion 3D objects.

There are metal working 6-axis machines that are very accurate. Once you design something, you could potentially reproduce it millions of times over exactly like first. (Not really millions because you'd get tool wear and other things that will change the precision.)

CNC is subtractive, it involves cutting pieces away. 3D printing is additive, which means it makes things by adding material.

Me: Thanks for explaining. Both sound cool.

Relevant bunny trail:
RR Industrial Arts Teacher: If you want to learn more about CNC, look up Titan.

He was a professional boxer, but he's become big on educating people about CNC through online courses and videos.

In one video, he highlighted German manufacturing. They respect manufacturing, so they have apprentice programs where young people learn how to work machines that cost millions. People make good money and have great careers in manufacturing. Others pay a premium for German manufacturing because it's a cut above the rest.

Parts of jet engines require a high skillset to make well. We (Americans) are ignorant of what it takes. It can take a few years to train a kid to work a machine well enough to create jet engine parts. You need programs in place for that to happen.

This is a cultural issue and the heart of our problem.
- We're ashamed of manual work.
- We value scientists, finance people, and sports stars.
- The top mathematicians take their skills to Wall Street instead of concentrating on research.
- We're told to teach leadership. It's all about that all the time, but then, we forget to teach people how to follow. You can't have all leaders. They'll make a mess of things and get nowhere.
- Following, cooperating, and understanding how to work together are vital skills missing from our schools.

Me: I can tell you're passionate about that. And you certainly have a lot of awesome points. We should return to this thread later.

So, you got the fancy CNC machine you asked for. What happened then?

RR Industrial Arts Teacher: First, we had the machine, but no software. I also had a really hard time getting the machine in place. It weighs thousands of pounds.

Schools are the absolute worst purchasers. They use antiquated policies and nearly always end up paying the highest prices. I found some workarounds and got good prices because I knew people. The policies are born as a response to corruption, but they still stink.

Took a month to get this machine up and running. I had to hire an outside source for $1000 of the school's money just to move the thing into place. It's a heavy, temperamental machine. (But I love it.)

Took longer to get it calibrated. There were too many kids registered for the course, so they didn't get time on the machine. The whole point of having the machine is to let kids build and create physical stuff, not just digital models.

Anyway, then Covid happened, and it knocked the pins out of education.

Me: Ah, a dark time in education.

What did you do in response to the pandemic/hybrid teaching?

RR Industrial Arts Teacher: I was kind of beside myself.

We got thrown out of school in March of 2020. I had 50 incomplete rocking chairs sitting in my shop. I offered to help the students finish them at home, but only some of them took me up on that.

Even this past year, I had kids fixing chairs from the previous year if they had extra time.

Most of my colleagues found videos and made up ten-question assignments. I didn't want to do that, so I learned how to edit videos and made a series of machine safety videos.

Students had to get a 100 on safety test before they would be allowed to touch the machines.

Hybrid was a mess. Kids coming and going all year long.

Me: Whoops. We're out of time again. Darn. That was fast. Hold that thought. I have a feeling you can elaborate a lot more on the pandemic/hybrid days.

Takeaways:
- The pandemic was especially challenging for classes like industrial arts, which are designed to be almost completely project-based, hands-on.

Challenges often force us to learn new skills.

Chapter 10:
Episode 130: Special Guest: Recently Retired Industrial Arts Teacher Part 3 – Creativity and Conundrum

Introduction:
Dear Reader,

We were right in the middle of Recently Retired Industrial Arts Teacher's account of how he handled the pandemic. He got to explain the situation in his shop but didn't tell us much about his answer to the whole not-being-in-school thing.

~Ann

Tell us more about your pandemic response.
RR Industrial Arts Teacher: Kids need to do projects. That's how we learn. You don't learn this stuff from a book.

I remembered that when I was in college, the art department had made furniture from cardboard.

So, I developed projects for students to tape or glue together at home. (It was a LOT of work.) I had to design the projects, test them, build a prototype, and refine it so I could adequately describe it to my students.

What kinds of things did your students make out of cardboard?
RR Industrial Arts Teacher:
- Catapult
- Bench
- Bookcase
- Gaming chair – that was a big project

What did these projects teach your students?
RR Industrial Arts Teacher: They learned how to follow a plan, and how to work with a new material (cardboard). They also learned that they could make a practical item from an easy-to-find substance. Building also involves skills on measuring, plotting, scaling up and down.

I took it easy on the kids in terms of time constraints. I gave them a lot of time for each project.

Hybrid—being in and out of school—was better but still kind of a disaster.

I'm proud of my accomplishments, but by the end I was toast. It's a physically demanding job.

How so?
RR Industrial Arts Teacher:
- You're on your feet a lot.
- You have to be aware of everything happening in the shop. The kids are often at different parts.
- You can't let the kids bully you.
- You have to find ways to connect with students.

I used to tell them every time they walk in they need to have a goal. Those goals may not be the same. One kid will be reworking their math. Another will be designing. Another working a machine.

What value did your students get from the course?

RR Industrial Arts Teacher: Tons. Woodworking and other industrial arts classes often benefit those who are less academically inclined.

These kids might be earning C's in their other classes. The way the school system is designed, they've heard a steady message of *you're just not as good as others* because the system favors book knowledge.

In my class, these kids got individual instruction. They could learn at their own pace. It's a thrill for those who aren't used to academic success to craft something that has value.

I've had kids come back and say things like your class was the only thing that got me through high school.

It's a haven for them. Their parents are used to getting bad calls from teachers, so it's especially gratifying when the student comes home with a mantle clock or full-size rocking chair.

Building stuff allows the kids to make something tangible that they're proud of. It demonstrates something they're successful at. They may not be mathematicians, but they're good at building things with their hands.

What were other projects you had your kids do?

RR Industrial Arts Teacher:
- Grandfather clocks
- Cabinets
- Bookcases

What value do you think industrial arts courses in general offer society?

RR Industrial Arts Teacher: This type of education is extremely important, but it goes unrecognized.

We think we're highly educated, but we don't know how stuff is made. It's critically important to understand process. We don't care much about plumbing, electricity, roofing, or air conditioning until we need those things.

There's value in manufacturing.

- Without manufacturing, you lose the creative edge.
- By building, you get the technological edge to keep improving.
- Shows that there are career opportunities that don't fall under the core academic classes.
- Shows the uses and limitations of machines. (How fast do you need to feed a router to get the machine to work its best? What's the goal of the machine? What materials work best? What kind of production quality will you get? What is the life of a particular tool?)
- You can't apply how something works until you've worked with it.

Putting tools into people's hands is important. There's support for music and fine arts. Most students aren't going to go make a career out of drawing or painting, but by enabling them to take courses to further their skills in those things, you've enriched their education. There's more to life than numbers.

Industrial arts are unrecognized.

Why do you think that is?
RR Industrial Arts Teacher: Everybody in administration has gone to college, so that's their frame of reference. That makes garnering respect for the field an uphill battle. Having a good boss helps, but it's only a start.

Back in the day, engineers would take a design to the guys on the factory floor and get them to help improve the machines and the process. We've lost that creative edge.

Experience brings that knowledge. I tried to give my students many experiences.

A suburban school like this would send plenty of kids to engineering careers without any practical knowledge.

Me: That's sad. Also, scary.

RR Industrial Arts Teacher: We're also hurting a segment of the population. These kids are told that college is the one and only road.

One time, we went on a fieldtrip to an automotive school. The kids were excited, one young man in particular. He wanted to make that his career. His parents didn't support him.

I've seen many of my students attend a community college, then drop out completely.

If that student had gone to automotive school and finished, he'd be making $70-80,000 a year now, but he doesn't because he got talked out of tech school.

There's a prejudice against not going to college. Just because you go to a tech school. Doesn't mean you can't get college credits. You can do that too. Take management classes.

There's nothing wrong with college but sending out a steady message of this is the only way is detrimental to many students. I've had other students tell me that they tell their guidance counselors they don't want to go to college but every meeting ends up starting the same way (what are your plans for college?).

Takeaways:
- Industrial arts classes are undervalued.
- College is an excellent path, but it is not the only path.

Chapter 11:
Episode 131 – Special Guest: Recently Retired Industrial Arts Teacher Part 4 – Past and Future

Introduction:
Dear Reader,

We've been all over the place with this guest.

This Chapter will be a bit of a recap, trying to piece together the life lessons he learned from a lifetime of living, working in sales, and teaching.

~Ann

Did you have friends in high school?
RR Industrial Arts Teacher: Yes, Freshman year was the worst year of my life, but Sophomore year, I made friends. We all loved chemistry and photography club. Still keep in touch with 1 friend from high school.

Me: Yay. Chem buddies.

RR Industrial Arts Teacher: I took a second year of chemistry and worked a couple of jobs. I did good academically, but I didn't like sitting still. I think I could have been a great lawyer, but the thought of reading and writing that much freaked me out.

Science was interesting, but my math skills were weak.

I probably could have done it, but I didn't know what to do. Tried accounting, and that didn't work!

Came to idea of industrial arts teacher because I loved making stuff in shop. In high school, I worked for a contractor.

Were you close to any teachers?

RR Industrial Arts Teacher: Got close to the chemistry teacher. He used to do wedding photography too, so he did our wedding. My wife was in his homeroom one year. (She didn't talk to me back then. I was kind of a nerd.)

Why did you try teaching?

RR Industrial Arts Teacher: Fell into it. Liked it.

What's the best, worst, and most fun part of teaching?

RR Industrial Arts Teacher:

- Best part is when you realize that you've impacted somebody's life and altered it for the good. They may not realize it for years, but it's great to be that positive influence in their life.
- Worst part is the constraints of teaching what I did. Because it was undervalued, people didn't want to put the necessary money into it.
- Worst part (take 2) Occasionally, you get a student you just can't crack. That's frustrating.

- Most fun is working with teenagers. They can be frustrating for a variety of reasons, but they are the funniest people on the planet.

High school made a bigger impact on me than college.

I went into teaching partly because you get to be a part of this pivotal point in teenagers' lives.

Why did you retire from teaching?

RR Industrial Arts Teacher: It was time to quit. I'm getting older. It's a physically demanding job.

- The room is 45' x 90'.
- There's lots of noise.
- You have to constantly be on the kids because they're teenagers not used to working on machines.
- Keeping them on task takes effort.
- They're also very good at ignoring you or tuning you out.
- There's a constant flow and fast dynamic with kids doing many different things at once.
- Time went fast, but I had to think on my feet a lot.

Age just began catching up.

I didn't want to keep at it just to put in years to get the pension. I know some people have to do that, but it just wasn't what I wanted.

Are you enjoying your retirement?

RR Industrial Arts Teacher: I'm not thinking of that yet. It's probably going to hit me in September.

Me: That's when many East Coast school start.

RR Industrial Arts Teacher: During most summers, I'd be in and out of the school doing maintenance on machines and planning new parts of the program.

I'm still sort of working this summer. I'm teaching my successor how to teach CNC class. He's taught before but not that class.

I'd also bought a cleanup bell because my students always need five minutes to cleanup sawdust, put away projects, and such. Since I'm the only one who knows how to program it, I got asked to do that. I also needed to pass the knowledge on so somebody else can program the bell.

What does life after teaching hold for you?
RR Industrial Arts Teacher: I'm not sure. Work's always been a constant thing for me. My wife is also retiring at the end of August.

I've done commercial work before, but I'm not sure I want the burden of running a small business.

I want to find something that has meaning beyond making a buck. Also working through Medicare and other paperwork junk. That's practically a fulltime job. The slightest variation in the way you fill out those papers can cause huge problems.

Me: I'm sure I'll be there before I know it. Ick. Paperwork. Also, I had the displeasure of being on a government website today. It was a study in frustration and inefficiency. I can only imagine what wonders medical websites hold.

Do you have any advice you have for new teachers?
RR Industrial Arts Teacher: Teaching has become difficult. Headwinds generated by administration—rules, regulations, things that you have to do—are trying to take away the creative control you have in the classroom.

It's not evil per se, just the trend of modern society.

More technology lets admin exert more control.

When I started in sales, there weren't cell phones. I had the freedom to be creative. By the time I left, technology had progressed to include cell phones and laptops. That translated to more oversight. We were inundated with emails because those at the top wanted complete control.

I had an epiphany one day. Everybody in sales does an annual forecast. This is your prediction about what you think you can sell in the coming year based on the past one. This helps to direct what gets made, how much gets made, and areas where the business will grow.

Anyway, after I gave my forecast one year, an opportunity arose. This let me crush the forecast. (I made a lot of sales.) Usually, this should be a good thing, but I was chastised for not meeting the forecast.

That's when I knew that the company had gotten too big. They would rather I have sold less product because it would let management appear to be in control and able to predict the future. It's beyond stupid.

The same thing is happening in education. There's such a burdensome emphasis on goals, IEPs, and other things that are about controlling every aspect of the kids' education.

My advice:
- Listen to the kids, parents, and other teachers.
- Teaching may not be a high-paying profession, but it can be an outlet for tremendous creativity. Joy is the creative outlet, but if you take that away, you're a drone.
- For every challenge that arises, find a way around it. (I.e., make cardboard furniture)
- Find a way to connect with students that fits your personality. I didn't directly correct students if I found them working at a bizarre angle, I'd make a joke about my friend Mr. Gravity. They'd get the point.

You've taught at—and attended school—at many different times. How has education changed over the years?
RR Industrial Arts Teacher: I went to a large high school, about 4,000 kids.

We had a college prep program, a business program (steno, typing, computer science skills, etc.), a general program for those not academically inclined, and vocational school (metal working, welding, woodworking, carpentry, electrical engineering, automotive studies, beauty school, culinary, etc.).

Woodshop could be taken by anybody. I appreciated the organization. It made sense to offer students many career paths.

These days, it's college or nothing.

There are so many great tech careers that would be better suited for some of these students.

Automotive school has almost no homework. The students get there and work early morning to afternoon. It's learning by actually doing the work.

Opportunities are great, and the money is there. It's the interest that's lacking.

I get annoyed that as a country we don't have qualified people to work manufacturing jobs because we've trained them all to believe there's no value in such work.

Takeaways:
- Find a job you love, be it academically inclined, creative, or practical and labor intensive.
- There are many solid careers that don't involve college.

Skilled labor has a lot of value.

Chapter 12:
Episode 132 – General Opinion: Back to School – Anxiety and Excitement

Introduction:

Dear Reader,

Several people have asked me if I'm excited to return to school.

I don't blame them at all, but the answer's a bit more complicated than a yes or no. I want to say yes, but I am aware there's a lot of work that must be done before we reach opening day. Not excited for that part.

In an effort to make this not completely about me, I have also asked a few other teachers to share their thoughts. Since it was a group of Christian teachers, I opened it up for them to share what's on their heart, including prayer requests.

~Ann

Do you get anxious?

My sample size was super tiny, but most said yes.

Some prayers (no particular order):

- Energy
- Encouragement
- Peace for the coming year
- Not growing weary or complacent
- Being a light; not being negative in any way
- School staff – wisdom, blessings for doing their jobs well
- Students – open hearts, open minds, whatever's going on in their lives that could potentially stand in the way of learning

Things that happen every year:

- Professional development/staff meetings – It's part pep talk, part refreshers, and part here's what's new in education.
- Online training videos – My state requires upwards of six-and-a-half hours of online trainings. While it is good information, it's absolutely soul-draining as well. Some schools do these corporately. Others, just assign it to be done by a certain date.
- New schedule – Some years you get all of the same type of class. Other years, you have three preps (classes to prepare lesson plans for).
- New classroom norms – You want to establish a comfortable learning environment quickly. If you want to implement something like a cell phone holder, that has to happen day 1.

Relevant aside:

Education is one of the few professions where the product is dependent on the performance of others.

For as much as they talk about students being more than numbers, their next breath with be data, data, data.

I get both. It's just difficult to balance the need to have measurable results and reach every student where they're at socially, emotionally, and academically.

Possible stressors:

- New policies and procedures – Much is the same, but schools are forever trying to improve. (In that sense, it's a discouraging career because nothing's ever good enough. It's always what could we do better. That can kill motivation.)
- The public schools aren't always in control. The state and federal governments also make many demands about what students need to do to prove they're successful.
- Parent communication – You want to establish this quickly too so that the first communication isn't when something's gone wrong.
- Learning new students – They come with a wide variety of situations and emotions.
- Getting school legs back – Summer schedules may not have the same demand for being on your feet for long periods of times.
- Change – Even if you teach exactly the same thing you did last year, there could be shifts in your duty schedule, your room assignments, or colleagues.

What often differs year to year:

- Students – Getting students to move on to the next grade is sort of the goal, so the oddity of getting a student back for a second crack at a certain subject is the anomaly.
- Staff – People come and go for many reasons. Some get nonrenewed (not offered a new contract). Some move away to take care of family or because a spouse's job moved.

- Room assignments – Schools apply for grants and do massive renovation projects. They knock out walls, combine classrooms, and shuffle teachers about.
- Some procedures – This year, it's a shift in how the kids are supposed to go to the restroom. They are attempting to cut down on the amount of random hall wandering and bathroom conferences happening.

Emotions that (can) crop up:

- Anxiety – so much to do, think about, plan, prepare for, etc.
- Excitement – The stuff listed above can be exciting too.
- Sad – Summer offers a big change of pace. This past summer was crazy busy, but it's a different kind of busy than a school year.
- Relief – It can be nice to return to a routine.

Things I bought/soon will buy/have bought in the past:

- Eraser caps
- Cell phone holder – This is new to me this year. The constant battle to deal with phones is wearying.
- Batteries – Always handy to have some on hand.
- Pencil sharpener – I already have one, but I can't find the cord to the other one and it was sort of dying anyway. It's probably time for an upgrade.

Note: I know we've had a previous discussion about what people buy for their classrooms. I also know many have very strong feelings about teachers spending their own money to get supplies. I buy them because it's more convenient to do so. I could get most things from my school if I had the patience to wait until next year.

Personal to-do list:

- Create class lists – I'm sort of old school in that I take daily attendance on a paper copy as well as put it into the computer. I like the option to refer to a paper. Besides, it helps with looking up grades if I'm away from my computer. (Let's be honest, that's a rarity.)

- Create classroom folders to hand things back
- Finish online trainings
- Organize backpack
- Set up Google Classroom
- Update the back-to-school survey
- Update the personal presentation
- Sign up for the online textbook
- Do some training with the new textbook
- Take updated notes using the new textbook
- Familiarize self with new testing platform
- Lesson plan for the first three weeks
- Proof and update policy sheets

This year, I have two different types of classes to prepare for. Since they are in the same content area, they're very similar, but I still have to have separate policy sheets.

- Update website
- Create student lists
- Create parent lists
- Write first letter to students and parents
- Organize desk – At the end of the previous year, I shoved everything into my drawers, so I had to unpack the front desk and make it pretty again.

Note: I'm not an elementary classroom teacher, but room setup is a big thing for them.

Conclusion:
Everybody is going to have a different set of rituals for preparing for the new year. The way I do things may create more work for me. I'm okay with this. It's methodical predictable work. While

time-consuming, it becomes a way to mentally prepare myself for the launch to a new school term.

Takeaways:

- Anxiety, excitement, and a mix of both are all valid reactions to the prospect of returning for a new school year.
- Whether you spend money on school supplies or not is up to you. (Don't go into debt for anything, but if you want a particular pencil sharpener, go for it.)
- Everybody's to-do list will differ, and that's okay.

Chapter 13:
Episode 133 – General Opinion: Notable Incidents that can Throw the Week Off

Introduction:

Dear Reader,

I'm sure every teacher can tell similar tales.

These are the sorts of incidents that can throw a day or a week off.

Here are two I heard about recently.

*For obvious reasons, I'm posting them anonymously to protect the people and schools involved.

~Ann

Incident 1: Cyber Crimes

Dear Ann,

This week started out odd because we had a day off right in the middle. I usually try to do some catchup on such days. Whatever I was doing wore me out enough to make me want to nap.

Anyway, I checked my phone when I woke up.

What do I see?

A missed call from the principal. I also have a voicemail message that just says: Call me.

Never good. Also, for the record, terrifying.

So, being a rip-the-bandage-off sort of person, I call this man back ASAP.

He tells me to get on Google Classroom and check for anything weird or inappropriate.

Apparently, one of the students on my roster has had their email account compromised, and somebody has been sending students offensive emails and posting inappropriate things on various teachers' Google Classrooms.

The principal ends with a *just let me know if you find something* statement.

Still half-asleep, I hop onto Google Classroom.

And find a highly disturbing picture along with a stupid message. I wouldn't repeat the message even if I could remember it because nobody needs to hear that nonsense. Suffice to say the person seemed to be a fan of Hitler.

I didn't see the message sent to the students, but I heard it was along the same lines, minus the sexual nature of the image I got surprised by and plus something more antisemitic.

~Tired Teacher

Incident 2: Loss in the Community

Dear Ann,

Me again. As if this week wasn't weird enough, this morning we got an email notification that there will be an emergency faculty meeting in a few minutes.

Not good.

I am lucky to have been reading email at the time or I likely would have missed it. Reading email in the morning isn't something I make a habit of unless I really have a lot of spare time after board setup and other daily prep.

Found a teacher friend I know is always in the school before me. (Sometimes, she beats the maintenance people there.) Let her know to check her email and walked down to wait for the meeting. Principal got straight to the point: a recent former student committed suicide. (He said the name, of course, but it wouldn't mean much to general readers.)

You know that cliché about there being an audible gasp filling a room? Pretty sure that happened.

I did not have the student in any of my classes, but I taught one of his brothers. I believe that family had several boys go through the whole system.

That means a lot of teachers had this kid.

The principal got choked up while making the announcement. He also said if anybody needed coverage to stop by the office and let them know. They would make it happen.

That was a strange morning.

There was an eerie, emotional atmosphere hanging over the school. Quite a few teachers were in tears or struggling mightily against them.

***

A week later, they arranged to honor the family at one of the football games and have people wear black printed versions of the kid's number. He had been captain of that team not so long ago. Suicide.

Such a simple word to encompass a horrible event that devastates families and communities.

That is all.

~Really Tired Teacher

Me: I'm sorry you had such a lousy series of events to deal with. Suicide is a tough topic.

We truly do not know all that goes on in a person's life. In most cases, we don't know the circumstances that lead to the decision to check out permanently.

Life is difficult, and stress comes in many flavors.

People die for many reasons, including disease and accidents. Each kind of incident has a different brand of pain.

Suicide is especially devastating because it seems sudden, even if there are a ton of warning signs.

There's not much advice I can give besides support people as best you can as often as you can.

A positive message won't solve everything, but it can't hurt to let the people around you know you care about them.

Closing thoughts and takeaways:

- School communities will experience loss.
- You matter to many more people than you think.
- Your life is connected to many, no matter how alone you feel.
- Cherish your loved ones and let them know they are loved and appreciated.
- Perspective is important. Many things in life will seem like they can't possibly get worse. It won't stay that way. There's a natural ebb and flow to life events, both good and bad.

Chapter 14:
Episode 134 – Special Guest Mrs. R.
Writer and Middle School Humanities
Teacher Part 1

Introduction:

Dear Reader,

Today we get to meet a writer and Middle School humanities teacher.

Yeah, I happen to know a lot of writers and made a point of asking the ones who happen to be teachers to answer a series of interview questions. The entire process has been fascinating.

Writing pairs well with school because it helps with processing everything.

~Ann

What would you like to be called?
Mrs. R.
Me: Sounds good.

Did you have friends in high school? What was your schooling like?

Mrs. R.: Yes, when I was attending school we had a three-room school for grades K-8. There were no public high schools, but we had two private schools that served as our public high school.

All classes were integrated, and the emphasis was on trying your best, less than standards.

I also chose a small college. So, I moved from 48 students, to 425, to 2500-ish.

Relationships between peers was huge, but also, the relationships between students and teachers. We saw the teachers/admin/support staff as real people despite there being a line of authority between students and teachers.

Did you get close to any teachers when you were a student?

Mrs. R.: I had a number of teachers that I admired and a couple I really just had no respect for.

The teachers that knew their stuff and could figure out a variety of ways of teaching to reach everyone while still carrying on "normal" conversations about "real" things were my favorites.

Honestly, I really liked the sarcastic teachers too, so it always bugs me when administrators tell teachers not to be sarcastic because adolescents don't understand sarcasm.

There can be some big social misses, but those are usually the same kids that miss the non-sarcastic cues, too.

Don't punish us all because of the few.

Me: Agreed. I think there can be good learning opportunities about communication there. Sarcasm is practically an art form. There's an instinct one develops about when and how to deliver. In the case of the few misses, you can usually clear things up.

I think the problem comes in when kids don't get it, internalize it, interpret it wrong, and then try to tell a parent about it and the message gets further lost.

You mentioned having taught before. What did you teach the first time? Are you teaching the same thing?

Mrs. R.: I volunteered in the schools for years and subbed for a variety of subjects and ages. I also led activities in the After School Program.

The first school I taught at I was the Humanities/General Ed teacher for boys grades ~5-12. These were students who had been removed from public school and were all over the place in terms of their knowledge.

Through the same school, I became just the Humanities teacher and no longer Gen Ed.

The next school was Middle School Humanities.

Then, I took two years off from primary teaching to work as support staff/coteaching in Special Ed.

I also took a year off to write.

Now, I am a Humanities teacher for grades 5-8.

Me: That first crowd seems tough. Those kinds of positions tend to have a high turnover due to stress.

Why return to teaching? (practical reasons, emotional reasons, etc.)

Mrs. R.: I returned for several reasons.

- On a very personal level, I couldn't work uninterrupted at home (writing/marketing), so I figured I might as well return to the workforce and get paid for my time.

- Paying off the mortgage early sounds delightful!
- But I also actually enjoy teaching kids.
- Helping kids find that lightbulb moment. They light up, and so do I.
- Giving kids skills for the rest of their lives ("transferable skills" being the big buzz phrase)

Me: Ah, buzz words/phrases. There could be many articles on current buzz words because they change every year.

Mrs. R.: Moreover, I returned to the school I had been teaching at ...

- So, I knew the team and the admin.
- I knew how desperately they needed a Humanities teacher.
- I knew I would be comfortable there.
- The commute isn't bad. And now I teach some of the younger siblings of kids I had before. That can lead to fun conversations.

Me: There's lot to be said of knowing what you're getting into.

Mrs. R.: I was gone just long enough to forget how hard it is to time manage the ridiculous number of things required of every teacher ...

- Leading random SEL lessons (Social-Emotional Learning)
- Confirming how kids are departing school
- Paperwork
- Cleaning the classroom
- Plan, copy, and grade (We get 45 minutes of paid time each day to complete these tasks.)

Did you have a different career?
Mrs. R.: I do a lot of things (often poorly, I fear).
- My family
- Writing

... are the two main focuses of my time outside of teaching. I think it depends on the day which gets the greatest focus.

This fall I have stepped way back on the homesteading. I'm not trying to make any extra income on it right now by baking or crafting.

- I intend to start crocheting some for holiday sales soon.

It's still a priority for me to be somewhat self-sufficient for our family.

- I cook from scratch most of the time, including a ton of meal prep on the weekends.
- Also, I just finished hanging our laundry outside to dry, for example.
- But posting on our homesteading blog, teaching classes, farmers markets—that I took a pause from.

I enjoy writing a great deal, but not so much the promoting.

Me: Amen to that. Yeah, promoting is the most annoying part of the writing gig.

Mrs. R.: I have been publishing on Kindle Vella and that has been a great experience. I love being able to publish a story while I write it!

I used to be good about writing a few weeks ahead of publishing and thus having time to edit well. Now I seem to be always in a rush and failing on that time buffer.

But I also enjoy having four ongoing series so I can always follow my mood for writing whether it be a sweet children's story, a nonfiction related to homesteading, or a fantasy romance.

A spin off from writing is the freelance editing and reviewing I do. The cool thing about freelancing is that I can work a whole bunch or not at all so my flexible schedule of it varies a great deal.

I'm sure I'll do more projects on vacations and summertime. Right now, I have some editing and ARC reviews to do.

Me: See the Author's note to find some of Mrs. R.'s writings.

Takeaways:
- Mrs. R. is a very busy lady.
- I'm pretty sure she'd do well in a zombie apocalypse. (Homesteading and cooking skills for the win.)
- Family is a priority for her.

Chapter 15:
Episode 135 – Special Guest: Mrs. R. – Writer and Middle School Humanities Teacher Part 2

Introduction:
Dear Reader,

Hi. The previous Chapter focused more on Mrs. R.'s background. Now, we'll dig deeper into her time as a teacher.

~Ann

Why did you choose teaching the first time? What circumstances brought you to teaching?
Mrs. R.: I had always intended to teach and to write for fun. Then, my college decided that I couldn't get a teaching degree and a writing degree. My response to that news was: wth???

Me: That's silly.

Mrs. R.: So, having to choose one or the other, I went with English/creative writing as it's more versatile.

I have used it for a bunch of jobs like writing up packages/vacation stays at an inn I worked at. Also, for book reviews. (I eventually started earning decently for some of those reviews.)

Me: Neat. I've done a lot of reviews over the years. Not many have paid well but I got some cool items out of the deal. This was back before Amazon tweaked their rules on gifting products.

Mrs. R.: When my children were very little I actively volunteered, then subbed and worked as support staff in the schools. It wasn't until I worked only in the office, away from the classroom that I realized how much I missed those connections and looked for a job full-time teaching.

What kind of school did you work in? Is this the same as before?
Mrs. R.:
- I worked in this same public school in the special education department before.
- Prior to that, I worked in a different small, public school.
- Prior to that, I worked in a private, all-boys reform school.

Me: That sounds about as varied as my teaching career. I think that just shows there's no wrong or right way to have a teaching career.

Some land in their forever school, and others bounce around a bit as life takes them into and out of the profession.

What is your current class load?
Mrs. R.: I have three classes, which sounds easy.

Me: Not really. Three preps sounds difficult to me. I only have two this year and it's making me nuts.

What does your school schedule look like?
Mrs. R.:

- I begin my day with a homeroom of seventeen 6th graders. Then, we move into an English Class of 45 minutes.
- Next, I have fourteen 5th graders for 45 minutes of English.
- After that, I have twenty-one 7th and 8th graders for 45 minutes of English.
- I then have a 45-minute planning time which is mostly used to meet with the special educator to modify the assignments.
- Then, in theory, I have a half-hour lunch break. Usually, it's a working lunch to photocopy, check emails, etc.
- Twice a week I cut it in half to do Book Clubs.
- My afternoon is three 1-hour periods of mixed English and Social Studies/History.
- I work in reverse order, beginning with my twenty-one 7th and 8th graders, followed by my fourteen 5th graders, and then my seventeen 6th graders followed by Homeroom.

Me: That might just take the cake for the oddest schedule I've ever seen, but I'm sure it would make more sense if I studied it.

Two months into school here, I'm starting to be familiar with my normal schedule.

When does the school run from and to? What kind of grades does it host?
Mrs. R.:

- We begin about the second to last week of August and go until mid-June.
- My school is PreK-8th, so our schedule is largely blocks/periods based on how to meet state requirements and to schedule lunches, use of the gym, art room, etc.

- Our Physical Education teacher, Art teacher, Music teacher, Violin teacher, and Nurse are all shared with other schools.

How long did it/does it take you to prep?
Mrs. R.:

- I come into school 45 minutes before the kids and stay 1-1.5 hours after the kids.
- I also grade and prep at home most evenings and at least one day each weekend.

How do you approach prep?
Mrs. R.: I am lucky in that all my students are 1:1 with devices so many assignments are loaded onto Google Classroom. I teach a mini-lesson, and then, the independent work is available to the students to complete while I help.

Therefore, my prep is collecting the resources, photocopying or searching and finding the information. We use no textbooks, so I spend a lot of time searching for mentor texts, examples, and sources.

Me: That sounds labor intensive but thank goodness for the internet. Google Classroom is rather convenient.

Mrs. R.: My focus is always to be as prepared as possible for my students so my grading falls behind. I always try to have a backup plan as well, because many of the useful sites I find at home are not allowed past the school firewall.

Me: Ah, yes, firewalls. Useful, but sort of a double-edged sword.

Mrs. R.: Differentiating for a wide variety of academic levels is tough. For example, one of my classes has reading levels that span from about 2nd to 6th grade.

Are things different now this round of teaching?
Mrs. R.:

- I have more support from my team for academic success this time.
- I'm also more confident in following student-led tangents to follow their interests.
- My overriding goal is to teach them to learn and thrive in life. That may or may not correlate with state testing scores, and I have finally gained enough confidence to not care.
- I care that they learn, not that they know the perfect way to solve test questions which has little to no bearing on the rest of their lives.
- Also, I have some great lessons saved in my repertoire now that I can tweak and reuse.
- That combined with working hand-in-hand with a special educator I have worked with before makes planning and implementing easier.

Me: You've brought up several key points, and I'm glad it's easier for you this round.

Takeaways:

- Teaching does indeed get easier once you have some lesson plans to pull from.
- State tests are a blah thing everybody has to deal with, but certain teachers like Mrs. R. care less about that and more about the students learning useful skills.
- Mrs. R. has students across a wide reading range.

Chapter 16:
Episode 136 – Special Guest: Mrs. R. – Writer and Middle School Humanities Teacher Part 3

Introduction:
Dear Reader,

In this Chapter, we'll get to some of the advice.

~Ann

How many prep periods do you get?
Mrs. R.: Previously, I have always had a second period prep if I had one at all.

This is the first time I have had a mid-day one.

On Thursdays this year, I actually have two (and not 7th and 8th graders for the morning period), but we have a team meeting for one prep.

Me: A "prep" that's a team meeting definitely doesn't count.

What is your favorite class to teach?

Mrs. R.: My favorite class really depends on the unit and my mood.

- This was the first year that I had my students learning narrative writing by having them use their research on a history topic to write historical fiction narratives. We're at the revising stage and it has been a lot of fun!
- I also really enjoy teaching history because we can incorporate a lot of projects and thus students can really show me what they understand.
- I start every Monday morning with a Creative Writing prompt. Sometimes, I can write along with the students, and sometimes, it's just a nice casual way to start the week.
- My 7th and 8th graders are the easiest to teach as they know how to learn. They have discovered that by working through the mini-lesson we move onto their independent or group work. Then, we might actually get free time. I am often able to bring them outside for a 10-minute break.

Me: Writing historical fiction in class does sound like fun. I bet that's also interesting for you as a writer (seeing what the kids can come up with).

What was your favorite topic to teach?

Mrs. R.:

- I'm enjoying teaching the students how to revise and edit right now. Which is ironic considering how tired I am of editing my own work.
- I also happen to know a lot about ancient civilizations and mythology, so those are the topics that I stress a lot.

Me: It's harder sometimes when it's our own stuff. We end up wanting to keep everything.

What was your least favorite class to teach?
Mrs. R.:

- Honestly, while I know it is important, I dislike the Social Emotional Learning classes, and the "Intruder" training we do.
- It very much depends upon my mood whether I enjoy leading book clubs.
- Class novels are notoriously not that interesting.
- This year, I have branched into some new sets. (One of which, I disliked almost as much as my students.)

Me: Ha. I think I became a writer because I didn't like the school books. But at least you could commiserate with them over the book being awful.

What is the best, worst, and most fun part of teaching?
Mrs. R.:

- Best: The best part, without a doubt, is seeing a student light up when they have a "got it" moment and that lightbulb just shines.
- Worst: The flipside is when you and a student just hit a brick wall, and they just don't comprehend something and you have run out of different ways to explain it. I'm more than willing to ask for help from their peers or mine, but often there's a delay before the understanding hits and we both feel frustrated.
- Most fun: When I can laugh WITH my students. Middle schoolers are incredibly witty. They are also awkward and thin-skinned, so it is important to build relationships first. But once they can completely relax with you and have fun, then I can have fun too. And the faces they make are priceless! Moreover, they are sarcastic as all heck and so

am I. I have to rein that in, because some don't understand hearing sarcasm, but I can always laugh about theirs.

- As I said above, I love projects. They tend to be far more fun than worksheets and are a great way for students to show understanding once we reach at least the middle of a unit.

Do you have any advice for new teachers?

Mrs. R.: I heard once that a woman doesn't really come into her own until she is in her mid-thirties, and she is fully confident by forty.

I hate gendered comments usually, but there is quite a lot of depth to this. And teaching runs a similar way.

- When we are younger, we try many new things, and we are often just finding our way in an unsure and feeble way.
- Then, we spread out to new levels in career or careers and family or whatever.
- But then, as our careers solidify or our children have thrived and become more independent as teenagers, suddenly we have time to pause, breathe, and realize that we are actually good at what we do, not just getting by.
- As this soaks in, we become more confident, and suddenly we are standing tall, confident, and relaxed.
- I tell every new teacher that with blood sweat and tears they will achieve their dreams or discover that they don't actually want this dream.
- They will have difficult days and great days. It's important to remember that.
- It's also incredibly important to develop a strong relationship with your team to hold each other up, learn together, commiserate together, and celebrate together.

Me: All great advice. I especially like the part that you acknowledge that the new teacher may realize this isn't the dream they've been looking for.

Never heard that saying before. I feel like I settled into my life/career late twenties. By then, I had a gameplan for getting the sort of teaching job I wanted to aim for.

Takeaways:

- Teaching may not be what some people pictured it to be. There's a lot of unseen and annoying nonsense to deal with on a day-to-day basis. That's not advertised well in the teaching programs.
- Teaching will have great days and very difficult days. I suppose that can be true in all careers, but it's more apparent in the teaching profession because it deals with young people.
- Strong relationships with your colleagues is very important.

Chapter 17:
Episode 137 – Special Guest: Mrs. R. – Writer and Middle School Humanities Teacher Part 4

Introduction:
Dear Reader,

More advice and thoughts on education as a whole.

Mrs. R. wears many hats. She's a writer, a teacher, and a mother. She's also held several other jobs within schools. Each role gives one a slightly different perspective on a matter.

~Ann

What do you think kids need to succeed at school?
Mrs. R.: As a society, we've gotten too caught up on teaching students how to test and not how to learn.

At the same time, we measure success by grades and not by ability. Therefore, we become too focused on helping every student succeed by providing accommodations.

And once we find those accommodations to help a few, we assume they can help all. Suddenly, we stop holding students accountable for self-growth, memorization, or independent investigation.

Me: Oooh, I should just print that out and frame it. That's one of the best summaries of the proverbial *problem with education* that I've ever seen.

Mrs. R.: While education was not perfect when I was in school, holding students accountable to the same level would be a drastic improvement.

Especially if we can find the compromise to help students have their needs met, when families can't, so that the student is ready and able to learn. Right now, students have learned that they don't need to learn.

Are you involved in any extracurriculars as a teacher?
Mrs. R.: While I am not involved in school or district extracurriculars now, I have coached cross country running in the past, and previously, I also worked in the After School Program which provided academic support as well as fun activities for two hours after school.

This year, I chose not to do either of those, in part because I need to pick up my youngest at his high school two towns away (there is no bussing option). Also, I skipped out on extracurriculars this year because my excess energy is focused on our homestead and my writing.

When do you think the emphasis on grades kicks in?
Mrs. R.: This has two parts.
- One part is the parents and their expectations.
- The other part depends upon each district.

Report cards come home from kindergarten and beyond.

To counter this and reemphasize learning, I also grade on participation as well as what they actually accomplish.

Many students can discuss a topic in depth and relate it to other things they know but cannot finish a project or paper to save their lives.

Always, I strive to teach the importance of individual improvement. From the beginning of the year, I tell students that I hardly care what level of reading they are at, I care that they improve their reading and their ability to understand what they're reading.

I am completely honest with these students and that helps me prep if they are at similar levels, but I'm willing to tailor the work to each of them so that they can learn at their level.

How did the pandemic affect teaching?
Mrs. R.:
- "Zoom" is a naughty word for everyone: students, teachers, and parents.
- Also, there are huge gaps in handwriting, complete sentences, and stamina.
- On the flip side, students are excellent at technology.
- As a parent and a teacher, I know there are some huge gaps of understanding for kiddos, but different ones for each kid in the class.
- We stumble into these holes during class and need to go back and backfill, to have solid foundations, but it's a lot of little gaps caving into big holes.
- Meanwhile, social skills were rough before and now largely non-existent for those struggling with that.
- The prevalence of social media is greater because that was the lifeline of social interaction for months for these students and continues to be so for them today.

- Teachers are so grateful to be in person and see our students body language and facial expressions in person to quickly gauge understanding now.
- It is so much easier to teach and see when to slow down or speed up based on what the student's body language shows us. That seldom came through the screen.

If you were given an unlimited budget and a year to make any changes to education systems/ your school, what changes would you make?
Mrs. R.:

I have been involved in schools as ...

- a parent
- PTO (Parent-Teacher Organization) member and president
- school board member
- Central office personnel
- support staff
- special education teacher
- regular ed teacher

I know that unequivocally the system is broken.

I honestly don't believe that it can be fixed but that it must be torn down and rebuilt. However, I don't think that will happen yet, so I'm here trying to make sure that my handful of students have the best that I can offer them.

With endless money, I would ...

- First strive to be fully staffed so that the adults and the students were fully supported. It's not only about the paycheck but the other benefits and support that must be offered to find the best educators and to retain those strong educators.

- Secondly, I would find a way for all schools to be spacious enough, safe enough, and supplied enough to fully, physically support learning.
- Thirdly, I would provide the time and funds for students to be able to have more hands-on learning as that is what they will remember in the years to come.
- Lastly, I would try to find a way to show appreciation for effort (not necessarily success) by students, educators, and families, and connect that with the communities.

I have no idea how to achieve most of this, but I sincerely do not believe that fixing our education system has anything to do with which books we have (generally) or which songs we use, or what style of paint is used.

The newest isn't always the best, nor is it that what has always been done is good enough. It is a whole package rebuild.

We also need to allow our educators to be people too.

They need to feel comfortable seeing families in the liquor store, at the movies, being creatives, being athletes, being whatever they want outside of school.

We need to let our educators have mental health days just as much as "sick" days. If we want educators who can energize our students, we need to energize our educators.

Me: I just want to hire you to speak at the board of ed meetings when they make silly policies about what days we can and can't take off unless it's an absolute emergency.

You also raise a lot of stellar points. I especially like the one about teachers being people with lives that exist outside the school.

Takeaways:

- The education system is broken, yet many teachers keep plugging away at their job so the few students under their care will get the best education they can.
- The pandemic was a rough time for many. It pretty much destroyed kids' social skills.
- Mental health days are as necessary as sick days.

Chapter 18:
Episode 138 – Tough Question: What Do You Do When You Have a Tough Class

Introduction:

Dear Ann,

What do you do when you have a tough class?

I know that's vague. Sorry.

I also know tough can mean many things, but by this, I mean most of the kids are nice but about 1/3 are just mean to each other, rude to me, and get in a self-righteous little huff over everything.

I don't like them.

When they asked me if I like them—by the way, stupid question— I may have confirmed they were not my favorite. Ask stupid questions, get stupid answers. This ain't rocket science.

First, my opinion of liking/not liking should have 0 impact on their lives. What does it matter?

If they want to be liked, they need to work a heck of a lot harder at being likable.

Teachers aren't complicated. We like people who listen to directions, aren't rude, and try their best.

Anyway, so, had an incident today.

The incident:
I had given a fluff project to give them a bit of break from the normal mentally heavy stuff we do.

They were supposed to present the project. (It would have been a free grade. Do it = you get points.) We also would have done a fun lab. But they pitched such a fuss over the presentation thing that I canceled the presentation and the fun lab.

They asked why.

I said because they've said they don't want to. Fine. They're a bunch of ... and left it at that. Actually, put my head down at that point.

Some of these little suckers went crying (figuratively) to the principal saying I called them a-holes.

Were they being a-holes? Yes. Did I call them that? No. Did I come close to calling them that? Yes.

What happened?
Got another evil little letter from admin saying come down for a meeting and bring union representation if I want to discuss something that happened in a class.

Normally, those are terrifying. They're still a little scary.

But I knew exactly which period the principal was referring to. And at this point, I don't care.

I know I didn't do anything wrong.

Meeting went fine.

But I was basically told to hide my feelings better ... or better yet, just don't have the feelings. (implied)

- Just keep on keeping on. (Cool. Avoid the issue. Stellar plan.)
- Ask the admin to come in to observe the class more. (Uh, yeah, hard pass on that.)
- Was also told I should not take it out on the rest of the class by avoiding certain activities. (No. No. No. I absolutely get to choose which labs to do with the kids. If I can't trust them, there's no way in heck, I let them do fun labs. Classes for better or worse are all or nothing. Can't single out the trouble kids and bar only them from activities. That would make too much sense.)

So, back to my original question: what do I do with a tough class?
Sincerely,

~ Frustrated Teacher

Dear Frustrated Teacher,

Sounds like you had a lousy day. Sorry to hear that.

You raise an important question. I'm not sure there's a pat answer that will work in all situations.

Here are some random thoughts for tactics to try:
Note: There will be a variety here, so pick and choose ones that might resonate well with you.

- Pray for them (the good, the bad, and the hot messes), and pray for patience and wisdom.

- (Attempt to) focus on the good kids in the class. They tend to be ignored anyway. There will always be knuckleheads. Contain them as best you can. But pour your time and energy into those who will benefit the most from the effort.
- Try to reach the knuckleheads. For example, indulge their stupid chatter about fantasy football or whatever they're into. Try to find common ground.
- If there's a lot of correction involved, try to mention some positive things too. Yeah, this can be insanely difficult.
- Build trust where, when, and however you can.
- If you have the energy, implement a few changes. If you don't, carry on, but try to be vigilant about those troublemakers and shut them down fast.
- Divide and conquer. Work with the tough kids one on one. They're generally intelligent, reasonable beings when you talk to them individually. It's when they get in groups that there's a primal need to impress each other with idiocy.
- Try select self-care drivel things like calming music, exercise, meditation, spend time with family, etc. – eh, the point is do something that helps you recharge. The more emotional margin you have in general, the more patience you will have when you have to deal with challenging people.
- If there are communications issues, try to be as clear as possible. That's a given. People take things in differently. Use a variety of ways to get the message—whatever that may be—across to the students.
- It might help to use a sticker chart. Physically mark off the time you have to be there. When you make it to a reasonable milestone, reward yourself. It's not the ideal coping mechanism, but hey, you could get yourself some cool stuff.

- Remember: Nothing lasts forever. You are good at what you do. You like what you do most of the time. (If that's not true and you are miserable all the time, you're in the wrong profession. Abandon ship. Life's too short to waste it on things that frustrate you incessantly.)
- Perspective can help. Try to recall why you do what you do. Remember that the pandemic hit social graces very hard. It's taking some people longer than others to remember how to treat others. Doesn't make it right, but it does explain some of the rough attitudes that exist.

I'm sorry I can't be more specific. Truth is, every class has a unique personality. The method that clicks with one will not work on another.

~Ann

Takeaways:
- Contain the crazy if you can.
- Try general stress-relief tactics.
- Tough classes are inevitable sometimes.
- There are sweet kids in every class. Do your best for them.

Chapter 19:
Episode 139 – General Opinion:
Christmas (Holiday) Morale Booster
Part 1 - Basics

Introduction:

Dear Reader,

About to out myself if anybody from my school ever reads this, but I'm okay with that.

I initially went into the series with a pen name, so I could be completely honest with conveying my opinions.

The series is now linked from my website, so it doesn't exactly take hardcore detective work to find that I'm behind the series.

That said, I've also not included anything I wouldn't say to somebody's face if they were so inclined to listen to my thoughts on the educational arena.

In the time between Thanksgiving and Christmas, you tend to get hit up with several requests for thank you contributions for maintenance, secretaries, and so forth. It's nice, but it's also impersonal.

This Chapter is about a small, fun thing I do annually for my colleagues and school staff.

~Ann

Overview of what I do:
Phase 1: Purchase
- Buy fun size candy. I aim for pretty Christmas-y ones this time of year, but since I intend to wrap them anyway, it's not a huge deal if I can't find what I want.
- Buy some hard candy.
- Buy sandwich bags (or pull from my hoarded stash).
- Buy movie style boxed candy, Christmas fun candy, small gift cards, and lottery tickets.

Phase 2: Prep
- Parse out the fun size candy and hard candy into piles of about 7-8 pieces.
- Put the candy into sandwich bags. I prefer not having the Ziploc ones (the style, not the brand), but that's all I had on hand this year. It's fine. Just a tad harder to wrap.
- Add the bigger items to a numbered list. I.e., 1 Swedish Fish Tropical, 2 Chocolate Coal, 15 $10 gift card, and so on. Make sure this list is duplicated in a second column. (Usually, size 16 Tahoma font is big enough.)
- Print the list. Cut it in half to separate the two columns. Save one.
- Cut the half of the list apart into the numbers and stick the paper strips into random bags.

Note about numbers: My candy hauls typically come to about 60-70 bags of chocolate and 5 or so bags of non-chocolate stuff. The prizes typically comes to 33. So, roughly half the packages will have an additional prize.

Phase 3: Wrap/ package

- Around Christmas, there's usually plenty of wrapping paper within easy reach. I'm a nerd, so I buy fun paper like Turtles, Minions, and Star Wars.
- Fold and wrap the smaller packets of chocolate. If you're making separate packages for non-chocolate lovers, be sure to keep them in a different place. I usually save some of the larger candy bags to isolate certain candy. You can also distinguish by wrapping paper or other marks.

Phase 4: Signups and distribution

- I do signups but I also let people join at the last second. Mostly, it's so I make sure I have enough packages on hand. I've never run out. In fact, most of the time, I have quite a few left over, which is fabulous for my sweet tooth.
- You can have people come to you or stick them in mailboxes. Usually, it ends up being some combination thereof because people forget.
- When people come back to you with a tiny slip of paper, have your numbered list handy and cross out what's been claimed.

Sample Email Invitation:
Dearest faculty/staff acquaintances and buddies,

Short Version:
I really should just stop numbering these. It's gonna depress me in a few years.

Anywho, I was at ShopRite for milk and might have walked out with $179 worth of milk, (food, I did get food I promise), + candy, so, um, I'ma need you to sign up for some of this stuff. (In the real thing, I put the google doc link.)

Wrapping has not begun yet.

Long Version: (for those who are new-ish to this)
Hi, my name is REDACTED. I work in the science dept. I'm a candy addict/ connoisseur (thank goodness for spell check).

Around this time of year, there's a lot of fun candy in the stores. I usually buy a crazy amount to share with y'all.

It'll be wrapped in whatever wrapping paper I find around my apartment. Some will have little slips of paper (LOOK FOR THEM!!!!!) and come claim the extra prizes. If you win some, you need to pick it up LOCATION REDACTED. Preferably before the Winter break. I think Tues Dec 20th, I will likely be in my room all day long. You can come claim prizes last two blocks of the day.

If you have ques, please email. Toodles.

Note: This, of course, is in my writing voice. You'll want to write letters and prep a document that reflects you. That said, feel free to copy what you need of the idea, methodology, and letter inspiration.

Sample Google Doc:
Title: Mini-Christmas/Holiday Freebies Cause I Love Candy ...

Text:
Greetings,

Welcome to the (enter year) Edition of the Christmas/Holiday Giveaway. ShopRite had Christmas stuff before Thanksgiving, which is kinda wrong, but whatever.

If I can find the Christmas candy, you shall have pretties ... if not, you will have to deal with normal candy, but I do have wrapping paper to make it festive.

What is this and how does it work?
1. This lovely google doc is where you sign up by typing your name in the schnazzy numbered list below. Come to

(designated area) on assigned day.

2. If you get a slip of paper within the candy package, you get whatever prize the paper says you get.

3. At the end of the day, we (the royal we) are going to jump right to delivering these to mailboxes or offices if you don't have a mailbox.

4. I'm going to start prepping packages this week then let them sit in a bag and think about their life choices for a few days. Deliveries will happen the Tues/Wed before break. (I will send another email then.)

(Include a relevant timeline.)
How do I win?

1. Sign up.
2. Receive package ... Open package.
3. Check for a VERY, VERY TINY slip of paper with a typed prize (or slightly shadier hand-written missives with a prize written on it)
4. If you win, do a happy dance, then come see me to claim your prize.

What can I win this year?

- More candy! Bigger candy! Better candy! (Movie style boxes, bags found in the aisle of good things, extra unclaimed bags prepped for the normal giveaway that I'm trying to offload on the nearest victim/volunteer.)
- Lottery tickets (scratch offs, value varies)
- Gift cards (Panera, Dunkin, Starbucks).
- If you don't want to do gift cards, try money. The last few years, I've done messy $10 ($10 made by raiding my change purse, crumpled singles, etc.) and neat $10 (a $10-bill).
- Maybe Random stuff ... depends how much stuff I find around my apartment.

- Whatever random cake-y, probably bad-for-you yummies jumped me in Shoprite. (I got Oatmeal Creme Pies. And there might be Little Debbie Christmas cakes cause those are da bestest.)

Disclaimer: Completely random fun. No entry fee. You are the beneficiaries of my candy addiction. The sole reason for the signup is so I know how many packages to prep.

Who Wants In?
Sign up.

P.S. Y'all have editing rights to the doc so you can add your names. Try not to let the power go to your heads.

Takeaways:
- Small gifts can be a morale booster.
- I'd say this takes moderate effort and monetary cost, but you can scale up or down as needed.
- It's not an idea exclusive to schools. You could run something similar in almost any moderately sized office.

Chapter 20:
Episode 140 – General Opinion: Christmas (Holiday) Morale Booster Part 2 – Cost Breakdown

Introduction:
Dear Reader,

I mentioned the overall amount of the grocery store bill in the last Chapter, but that also included my weekly allotment of food.

In this Chapter, I'll give you way more details about cost in case you're thinking of trying something for your office.

~Ann

Stuff you need and probably have on hand (and estimated costs):
- Wrapping paper – I tend to get mine from Five Below, so it's usually $5 a roll.
- **Note:** There's an Easter version of this gift-giving idea that's slightly easier because there's no wrapping involved.

- Tape – scotch or packing. I keep a good supply of packing tape around, so I just used that. I get packing tape from Costcos. I think it costs around $16 (at least that's what the online cart thingy is telling me.)
- Scissors – also from Costcos. $11.39 (Please note, this also assumes you have a Costcos membership, which is like $50 a year.)
- Sandwich bags (around 100) – I had two packs of 50 store brand knockoff baggies on hand. I bought them when they were around $1 on sale.

Cost breakdown of the actual haul: (this will vary by year)

Note: This has worked for my school district, but yours may differ based on how many people you're doing this for. Prices are for 2022.

Candy for the initial packages:

- Lindt Lindor assorted $12.99 x 2 = $25.98. (I try to get something like this that's slightly bigger or better than other items.)
- Mars Mixed minis $10.99; I think this had Twix, Midnight Dark Chocolate Milky Way, Milky Way, Snickers, and 3 Musketeers
- Hershey's Miniatures $11.59 – $2.37 = $9.22
- Hershey's Kisses Christmas $4.29
- Hershey's Reese's $4.29
- Snickers Christmas $4.29
- Brach candy and mints $1.59 x 4 = $6.36
- Starbursts Reds $4.99

Cost estimate for this section: $70.41
Note: One of my colleagues is allergic to chocolate, so I usually make 5-10 packs for non-chocolate people.

Larger candy and stuff for prizes:

- $15 worth of lottery tickets (5 x $1 and 5 x $2)
- $10 gift cards to Panera, Dunkin, and Starbucks $20 (I have two $10 gift card prizes in the mix, but the people get a choice. My church sells scrip for these, so I tend to have a supply of them at the ready.)
- Skittles Gummies $4.99; I ended up with too many large candies, so I might have kept this one. (Translation: Munching on them now.)
- Riesen x2 ~$4.00 (I think it was on sale.)
- Wiley Wallaby's red licorice $2.99 (on sale!)
- Oatmeal Cream Pies $2.50 (I stuck these in an overpriced tin I bought from cub scouts. The tin originally had really crappy white cheddar popcorn in it. Somebody's gonna get the repurposed popcorn tin.)
- Haribo Twin Snakes $2.39
- Haribo Peaches $2.39
- Haribo Happy Cola $2.39
- Andes Mints $2.29
- M&M's crunchy x2 $2.20 (I think that was on sale.)
- Hot chocolate packs $1.99
- Junior Mints $1.50
- Spearmint Leaves $1.49
- Orange Slices $1.49
- Fruit Slices $1.49
- Swedish Fish assorted $1.29
- Sour Patch Kids tropical $1.29
- Sour Patch Kids watermelon $1.29
- Santa's Sack (chocolates, probably blah ones) $1.25
- Chocolate coal $1.25

Cost estimate for this section: $75.49-ish (came up 2 cents different on recount)

Fun fact I learned recently: Nevada doesn't have a lottery because of the casinos. They don't want the competition. So, I guess in Nevada you could do small cash prizes or other random candy bars.

Time cost breakdown:
Did the shopping while I was already in the grocery store. I believe I spent one afternoon sorting and bagging and two more wrapping the packages.

- Shopping ~1.5 hours
- Letter writing and doc writing ~0.5 hours (Your time will vary by how quickly you write. I'm also probably faster because I have old ones I can modify or have done this a few times and know what I want to say.)
- Sorting and bagging ~1.5 hours
- First round of wrapping ~2 hours
- Second round of wrapping ~2 hours

Estimated time commitment: 7.5 hours

Reflections and observations from doing this 9+ years:
- The monetary cost tracks. In the past, it's been around $100 for the candy and other consumables. This year, the estimate comes to $150, with rounding and assuming my math checks. (The math didn't include taxes. Candy is taxable.)
- Time investment is about a week prep. I suppose you could do everything in one day, but that might drive you nuts.
- People usually appreciate the effort.
- Don't go into debt over this. You can scale up or down as needed or cut the prize section altogether. It's way more fun with prizes though.

- There's usually some packages left over, so I get some candy to throw into my work stock. Sometimes, me, myself, and I get a lottery ticket out of the deal too.
- It doesn't have to be Christmas themed. I do a similar thing at Easter. You don't even need a holiday excuse to do this. Run one whenever the mood strikes.

Though this Chapter is about the cost of the endeavor, the spirit of the activity is small gifts for making people happy.

Takeaways:
- If you run it the way I do for a similar number of people, the money cost is around $150.
- The time cost is about 7 hours spread over a week.
- It's kind of fun to see that much candy all in one place. Bonus: There's usually at least one piece that gets sampled along the way.
- Personal rewards satisfaction. You get to spread a little holiday cheer.

Chapter 21:
Episode 141 – Anonymous Guest: Two Tales

Introduction:

Dear Ann,

Whenever my school does job postings, they send an email around to people in the district. This is done for both internal and external job openings. I think the idea is to give us a head's up in case anybody is interested in applying for the job.

That's often how you can confirm pieces of gossip like who's leaving and when.

Recently, we got one that confirmed a social studies teacher is leaving out district. The dates on the job posting tell me it's an immediate opening for a tenure track position.

I don't personally know the lady well, but I know the kids like her. Over the past few years, she's been very involved with the school community. I think she even started two clubs from the ground up. Naturally, that prompted musings of what happened. After minor investigative work (a.k.a. asking the people in the know), I've concluded there are two possible scenarios as to why she's leaving.

Yesterday, we received an email from the Superintendent that included some odd wording. It said something like the multi-school forum is not the place to air your grievances with the district. Of course, I asked some colleagues about that. They thought it had to do with something the woman said at such a meeting. Could be true. Could be false, but the email's implications are troubling.

It feels like we're being silenced.

I've heard the question raised at this group meeting was: what are some good and bad things at your district? If you take that question at face value, it feels like you should be free to be honest, but if the superintendent's email has anything to do with why this woman resigned suddenly, it doesn't feel so free.

In this scenario, the teacher went to this meeting, got asked the good/bad question, gave her opinion, and got in trouble.

The other possible reason might have to do with a kid. I won't quote anything because this account is many times removed from the source. However, my source was a student, so there's probably some truth to it. For some reason, the kids often know things way before the faculty and staff do.

In this scenario, a student said something completely inappropriate, and the teacher made an offhand comment. Fast forward, the child went to guidance and complained, the teacher got suspended, and then she quit.

When I asked one colleague which scenario she believed, she said the truth is probably somewhere in between, and the two incidents (if they even happened) compounded each other.

I don't know whether this lady is leaving the teaching profession or just leaving this district. Either way, I find the scenarios troubling. It feels like they don't trust us. I can understand wanting to put your best foot forward in public, but it feels wrong to ask for honesty then penalize people when you get it.

There's also very large double standards. Of course, teachers bear more responsibilities and should take care with their words, but suspension for a comment that a student felt was inappropriate seems way overboard. Again, I don't know the exact comments or context, but this isn't the first time I've heard: kid said X (nothing happened); teacher said Y, admin suspended a teacher scenarios.

Just feels like a heavy load to be carrying around the holidays. Even though it doesn't affect me directly, it's not great for morale. The administrators are all about rah-rah, we are behind you, we appreciate you, we support you, until it comes time to actually do any supporting. Is that a faulty perception?

I'm interested in hearing your thoughts. Should I be worried?

Sincerely,

Anonymous Teacher

Dear Anonymous,

Thanks for reaching out. I agree with your colleague who said that the reason for the teacher's sudden resignation is likely a combination of things.

It could be that these are the main two factors, but there may also be factors unrelated to these separate incidents that weighed in.

To your points, I'm reminded of the lovely harassment videos my district requires us to watch ad nauseum. It's something like for it to be considered harassment, the offended person doesn't even have to be the one being addressed. Honestly, I think that's a sign of sad things said about our society.

- Should people be free to be mean to each other? Of course not.
- Should people guard their words? Yes.

- Should one (or two) mistake(s) essentially cost someone their job? No.

I suppose how effective your administrators are will vary per situation. It sounds like yours are people pleasers, but I don't know enough details to say for certain.

It's completely valid to be extra cautious when it comes to giving feedback, even sought after feedback. Many times, people ask for an opinion with a preconceived notion of what they want to hear. They react poorly when your answer deviates from their expectation. It's easier to say "we want to improve" than to put in the work and make meaningful changes.

That's one possibility.

The other possibility is that the teacher in question truly said something out of line that unfairly cast the district in a bad light. No way of knowing.

Should you worry?
- About the general state of humanity? Probably.
- About your job? No.
- About your school? It's fine to feel concern for your school. It just means you care for the place. Whether by choice or by force, the community experienced a sudden parting from a member. That's worth noting. I don't like the phrase feel the feels, but it fits.
- About kids realizing the insane power your district hands them on a silver platter? Probably. But most kids are too self-absorbed to do much with it. And truth be told, every profession has terrible people to deal with. Only the flavor changes. Here, there is a small chance you can steer a few kids away from the path of being complete socially inept ninnies. (Lost track of the times I've had to tell my students

to be nice to each other. They are so ready to tear each other down. It's sad.)

Like vs. Love Aside:

I've been reflecting on this lately. It's the week before break and kids are losing their dang minds. It's like a full moon x 1000. They're ornery and combative and will literally argue with you over anything.

Told a kid he should get back to work. He said I was in his way. (For some bizarre reason, he was working at the back lab bench, so I was indeed in his way. Not the point. It's the attitude that came with the remark—combative, that's the problem.)

That makes them act the fool, more often than not.

You can love your students without liking their behavior. They often confuse disapproval with dislike for them as a person.

Takeaways:

- Breaks are made for teacher sanity as much as student sanity.
- There are multiple sides to any story.
- Guard your words.
- Sometimes, people ask for honesty when they really have what they want to hear in mind. Learning to predict that can save you some heartache.
- Sometimes, life and circumstances cause some opportunities to change. It sounds like the teacher who left is the sort who will land on her feet.
- Love and like don't have to go hand in hand. You can love someone without condoning poor actions, attitudes, or behavior.

Chapter 22:
Episode 142 – Anonymous Custodian: Tales from the Gross Side

Introduction:

Dear Ann,

If I told you everything I've seen over the course of my career, we'd need several days to cover them all.

I've found many things in the toilet, including an entire roll of toilet paper, a small toy, a pair of pants, and vape pods. The toy was from a kindergartener, so I suppose there's a reasonable assumption he didn't know the consequences of that action. The other three incidents were definitely done by high school kids.

The students get annoyed when the administration or custodial staff close the bathrooms, but we have to in order to deal with these kinds of incidents.

Speaking of bathroom woes. Once upon a time, the school had a problem with a young man who liked to use feces to write on the drapes. Besides being gross and unsanitary, it was highly inconvenient because we had to take down the drapes and send them out for official cleaning.

Why do kids do these destructive things?

I could write you a second whole volume based on stuff kids have written or drawn on the desks.

~Anonymous Custodian

Dear Anonymous Custodian,

First, on behalf of teachers everywhere, thank you for what you do. I would not want to do what you do.

Sometimes after project or lab days, the room is a downright disaster. I've spent some time cleaning up after them and retrieving my supplies, but I can't imagine having to pick up after kids every day.

It got worse during the pandemic because they let the kids eat in the gyms. I've had that duty several times. Even asking them directly to throw out their garbage has only marginal results.

Second, I'll admit I have no idea. Here are some random thoughts.

Some reasons for doing destructive things:
- Apathy
- Ignorance
- Boredom
- Amusement
- Short-sightedness
- Discontent/ Rebellion
- Satisfaction/ Control

Apathy:
When it comes to things that do not directly affect them, many people are apathetic. They just don't care.

They don't have to clean up, so why should it bother them? This attitude holds for their view of garbage. I can't tell you how many times I've heard "It's not mine. Why should I pick it up?" (Well, it's certainly not mine either, but here we both are. Make better choices in friends.)

If I recall correctly, there was a semi-recent article about some Japanese fans who attended the World Cup and went around picking up garbage for other people. The act was applauded as something abnormal and laudable. When interviewed, these people mentioned respect.

The entire concept makes me a bit sad.

I also recently heard of the appalling state some renters left their apartment in. I couldn't imagine living in such filth. Dust, yes. Filth, no. Things were broken. There were unidentifiable stains on the carpets. Apathy at its destructive finest.

I've had kids in my class have a wrapper of some sort and just chuck it at the floor. They've only thrown it out when I pointed out the error of their ways.

Ignorance:

This is probably the least offensive reason, though not a great excuse. The kindergartener who threw a toy in a toilet genuinely might not have known better. Correction and direct instruction and frequent reminders are best in that case.

Some kids need to be taught basic niceties because their parents aren't up to the task. There can be a whole host of reasons behind why such lessons aren't sticking or were never taught.

Boredom:

The forbidden has always been alluring, regardless of the context. Trouble is interesting.

That's why so many news articles focus on tragedies. Bored people sometimes feel the need to create trouble in an ill-guided attempt at generating something interesting.

Amusement:
Some people have a twisted sense of humor.

There's a fine line between practical joke and malicious intent. There are people who like watching the world burn.

Short-Sightedness:
If something doesn't have immediate rewards or consequences, some people can't see who or what is hurt or inconvenienced.

Discontent/ Rebellion:
Those who like causing trouble usually get this out of their system when they're young, but it can take a while.

Satisfaction/ Control:
Some kids think they have so little control over their lives that they love making trouble just to see how adults will react.

This is negative attention. It's a terrible excuse.

They can at least have the private satisfaction of seeing people scramble to adjust to something they put into motion.

What can we do to prevent such things?
The burden placed on the US educational systems aren't entirely fair. Nevertheless, if you don't want to have thousands of dollars in plumbing work done, you're going to have to make some effort to curb destructive behavior.

- Direct conversations about right, wrong, expectations, and consequences – may not have much effect, but it should at least prevent instances of repeat performances from those who fall in the ignorance category. You might even catch a few from the apathy category.

- Appeal to parents to address things with their kids – again, not foolproof, but it can help
- Alternative – Kind of controversial because it could be seen as condoning bad behavior, but providing a garbage can to throw whatever (specifically vape pods) might be the bandaid approach. It won't fix the problem at its source—ornery kids, but it might lower your plumbing bill.
- The long game – Well, you could inconvenience them. Close certain bathrooms; make them stand in line so only a limited number can occupy them at a time. It's hard to predict the effect of a plan like this. That would require a relatively sophisticated cognitive connection between behavior and consequence. (You risk having people upset with no idea why something is happening. Bathrooms are closed because they need to be fixed ... again. Stop throwing crap that isn't crap in the toilets.)

Takeaways:

- Custodians should be thanked at every opportunity. They do not get paid enough to deal with kids' poor choices.
- Fair or not, the education system should also strive to address character flaws and social gaps kids come with.
- Parents can be partners, though most of what we hear are the negatives.

Chapter 23:
Episode 143 – General Opinion: The Dark Side of Technology

Introduction:

Dear Reader,

We've already discussed (probably way earlier at this point) how much trouble phones can be in schools.

Now, let's tackle AI (Artificial Intelligence) and electronic cheating.

Scifi movies and other entertainment mediums have long spoken about the dangers of AI running amok, but the dangers in our present age are more about people sabotaging themselves with something that should be a helpful tool.

For the purpose of this Chapter, I'll keep the focus on education, but I've heard AI discussed in the writing world because of the debate over using it to create fiction, nonfiction, book covers, character art, and audiobooks.

My point is that the discussion is just getting started. People are going to have to learn to use AI ethically and having it used to cheat on English essays is a poor start indeed.

~Ann

Catching Cheaters on Google Presentations.
Some of Google's suite of stuffs can be clunky, but the history button is pure gold.

One of my colleagues said she made a Sophomore cry because she caught him cheating on a project.

He, of course, denied cheating, but she could see that his project had started identical to this other kid's project. The history let her see every change the cheater made, which wasn't all that many.

I'm often surprised by how many kids still get caught by this. Many teachers directly tell students about it in an effort to curb cheating from the start.

ChatGPT makes it easier for people to generate authentic sounding content.
This has caused a stir in academic circles because students are using it to cheat on essays.

So, what's the big deal? Isn't essay writing a pointless task anyway?
Writing is one of the major forms of information dissemination.
You could have the world's deepest, most profound thoughts, but if you can't get it into a form that others can understand, it's not going to have much of a life.

Sure, there are video mediums like YouTube and TikTok where you could just flip your phone camera on and say what you need to say, but the act of writing essays teaches you a way of organizing your thoughts.

I too ranked among those who suffered through high school English, essays and all. (Don't think I ever voiced that despised phrase: *When will I ever use this?* But I'm sure I complained at some point.) And then God, who has a wicked sense of humor, made me a writer.

Students have had search engines at their fingertips for many years, yet many don't have the wherewithal to use them. The mind is powerful but taking shortcuts can dull the senses. Learn how to write proper essays, then go your own way when you're older and wiser.

GPT-2 Output Detector: (An English Teacher's New Best Friend)

Note: They have a later version now.

Background: It's an open-source project (app) created by a Princeton student (Edward Tian) that helps detect ChatGPT generated information.

A colleague of mine recently used it to bust a student cheating on his physics assignment. Kid had the nerve to ask for proof the co-teaching pair caught him cheating, but we can talk about the poor attitudes in a different Chapter. (Bad attitudes are sadly becoming more common even in "good" districts.)

They entered his project work into GPT-2 Output Detector, and it came back with a report of 97% likely to be AI generated.

How does it work?

There are already articles on what this app is looking for, but essentially, AI-generated stuff has a pattern, just like any writer. People are more unpredictable than AI. This app essentially analyzes the degree of randomness.

Here's the thing. Everybody has a style. This is just a tool that confirms teacher's instincts. I've had kids cheat by copy-pasting stuff from the first article that pops on a Google search.

Know how I caught the cheater? The article used words that were well beyond this student's vocabulary and style. That made me Google a small piece and the article popped up with the student's presentation word for word.

Why do people cheat?

- Because they think it's easier than doing the work. Honestly, the amount of effort some people put into cheating is astounding, and sometimes, it's more than doing the original task.
- Because they don't see the value in the original task.
- Because they've gotten away with it thus far.

Why is cheating dangerous?

- The forbidden always has appeal.
- Getting away with cheating leads to dangerous mindsets.
- It's addictive. Rarely will someone just cheat on inconsequential things. Penalties for dodging a high school English essay might be a failing grade on the assignment and maybe a detention. But if you get away with it, then what? Things outside of high school carry stiffer consequences.

Cheating is not reported to administration all the time.

- Reporting Cheaters is annoying.
- The policies are rather black and white.
- There's a burden of proof to bear if you want to go with official channels.
- Those who cheat tend to be the ones that a 0 will hurt the most. Teachers often compromise on the policies because they genuinely do not want the student to fail. (If you fail the course, you have to either take summer school or repeat the course. Nobody wants that.)

Takeaways:
- Busting cheaters is initially satisfying.
- Teachers want their students to learn from the mistake, not repeat it.
- Technology is a double-edge sword. ChatGPT – makes cheating easier; GPT-2 Output Detector – makes it easier to catch cheaters using ChatGPT.

Chapter 24:
Episode 144 – Special Guest: A – Urban District Middle School English Language Arts Teacher Part 1

Introduction:
Dear Reader,

I think I've gotten to try every method of interview running within the last week.

Exciting but busy.

This one came about during a late-night Facebook messenger chat. Haven't done too many of this style, but there's a certain elegance to them because they're likely the most organic method possible. It's still written, so people have time to process, yet the questions come one by one and can flow into one another.

My friend wanted to be anonymous for her stint in a different project, so I'm going to go with the same codename this round: A.

~Ann

Me: (Sees a friend who interviews very well and happens to have a job that fits Dear Ann perfectly. If you feel like you dropped in to the middle of a conversation, it's probably because you dropped in to the middle of conversation.)

Would you like to interview?
A: Yes, I'd be happy to. What we went through with Covid was crazy. I teach ELA to 7th graders.

Me: Awesome. You can answer as much or as little as desired. I'll reorder as necessary.

Did you have friends in high school?
A: I was little miss straight A's.

Actually, that makes a little hard when I'm working with struggling students because I can struggle with why they don't get something, if that makes sense.

Me: It does. When we pick up on something easily, it's tempting to think everybody should have that ability.

A: I did have friends in high school, though I was not exactly super popular.

That kind of ties back to what I told you about my dad being a minister.

Small town stuff but kids didn't want what they were doing to get back to my dad so I got excluded from a lot.

Me: (We'd done an earlier interview that shows up in Chapter 7 of Dear Ann 3 – The Prayer Project.)

That too makes sense. I can see both sides. Seems silly to me, but then again, many things kids do can be inadvertently cruel to each other.

Did you get close to any teachers when you were a student?

A: I loved my math teacher.

He was such a nut. He looked like Albert Einstein and acted really eccentric.

I took all four years of math just to hang out with him even though math is not my thing.

Me: That is dedication.

How many years have you been teaching? Did you have a different career?

A: I think the teaching thing has been six years.

- Before that I spent 20 years in academic publishing.
- Before that I was a reporter then a desk editor at a daily newspaper for three years.

Me: And suddenly I want to know what being a reporter and a desk editor for a newspaper was like, but that's another interview I shall bother her for later.

Why did you become a teacher?

A: It's not a great or inspirational reason.

Educational publishing has been folding in on itself for a while. I would've happily worked in publishing forever, but more and more and more the work I wanted to do was being outsourced to places like India in the Philippines.

So, I was sitting around cutting purchase orders for other people to do my job. And they—the powers that be—were laying people off like crazy.

I didn't think there was enough career left for the amount of time I had between me and retirement.

So, I looked around to see what I could do with my existing degree, and that led me to the alternate route program for teaching.

Me: You brave, brave soul. (As a high school teacher, that is the sentiment I have for anybody who teaches elementary or middle school. Kids are crazy at those ages. Sometimes cute, but mostly just little packages of unpredictable emotions.)

Have you taught anywhere else?

A: No, I've never taught anywhere else.
Because I've been sort of meandering my way through different careers, I really am a relatively new teacher, even though I'm in my 50s.

What's it like teaching in an urban district? That must be something.

A: Yeah. It's definitely a whole different world.

Sometimes, it's completely heartbreaking, but other times, it's rewarding.

Me: I guess that could be said for much of the teaching profession, but the level of heartache and concern is different.

How did the pandemic affect teaching? And what are some challenges you face as a teacher?

A: There are so many I don't even know where to start.
- Before Covid I would've said lack of technology. But the huge blessing for urban students was that the school districts were forced to come up with 1-to-1 technology. So now all my students have their own chrome book. That has made things easier.
- We have very little in the way of resources or curriculum. So, we (the teachers) have to write and create and purchase and make copies. It's never ending.

- When Covid hit, it was like ... what do I even do? Our curriculum is supposed to be novel based. Meaning that we have paper copies of a few novels and we're supposed to teach all the standards based on those novels. But, when the kids are home and the novels are in the school, then what?
- I was purchasing the Kindle version of the books and projecting them on the screen and making videos of myself reading the chapters on Screencastify. And I was one of the lucky ones cause I'm fairly tech savvy.
- Meanwhile, this year, we're also working without a contract.

Fun fact about education: In the state where A works, the teaching contracts expire every three years or so. Some temporary ones get put in place to cover negotiation years where the negotiations aren't being resolved quickly.

To be *without a contract* means the teachers are working under the old pay scales. (No raises.)

Me: I did a little Screencastify, but I didn't fall in love with it. I'm happy to be teaching the normal way now.

What advice do you have for those considering your career?
A:
- Work smarter, not harder.
- Repurpose what you can.
- Find a way that works for you to be organized because there are endless details and responsibilities in this job.
- You have to keep a lot of plates spinning at all times. I understand why people might burn out. There is just so much to this job. I think it benefited me that I had an office kind of job first.

- A lot of the paperwork types of tasks are easy for me, but I know that that stuff can become quickly overwhelming. The lesson plans and the records for professional development hours and the grading and planning. It's a lot!
- And if you find yourself in a school with unsupportive administration, move on. It's not worth it!

Me: All excellent advice.

Did that happen to you? Have you worked for a school with terrible administration?
A: Yes.

- My first school in the district was absolutely hell. It was a tough school. One of the worst in the district. Like I was breaking up fights every day kind of bad.
- The principal was absolutely horrific. He knew the school was bad, so he spent his time trying to find ways to blame the teachers.
- And then they brought in a second principal who spent her time writing everybody up about things like bulletin boards.
- I can't even explain to you how bad that place was.
- I'm in a better situation now, although it's not perfect.

Me: I can imagine the blame game is fierce in tough districts.

Takeaways:
- Competent and supportive administration makes a huge difference in the smooth running of a school.
- Teaching involves a lot of things happening at once. Being highly organized helps.
- Being tech savvy can also help in modern teaching jobs.
- The pandemic was messy and awful in so many ways, but one small point of good that came of it was urban districts had to get the kids Chromebooks to do their schoolwork.

Chapter 25:
Episode 145 – Special Guest: A – Urban District Middle School English Language Arts Teacher Part 2

Introduction:
Dear Reader,

Join me in welcoming A back.

Haven't had the pleasure of speaking with many urban district teachers, so the interview was eye-opening in several ways.

~Ann

Are you involved in any extracurriculars as a teacher?
A: I'm not a coach or anything like that as far as extracurriculars go. That's probably a bit of a suburban thing. It's not like we've got a bunch of clubs or anything.

Me: That kind of surprises me, but I guess it makes sense from a lack-of-resources standpoint.

When do you think the emphasis on grades kicks in?

A: The *focus on the grades* thing might also be a suburban issue. My students are not focused on their grades.

How many kids are in the school you work at?

A: My district is a little strange. The school is a K-to-8 district. There are middle schoolers here, but the school itself mostly functions like an elementary school, which really sucks.

We've got something like 800 students in the building.

Probably a little less. Our count has been going down in the last couple years.

Why do you think the count's going down?

A: I'm not sure exactly.

We have students absolutely pouring in the door from the Dominican Republic. So, I honestly don't know why the overall count seems down.

What are some of the triumphs of teaching?

A:

- Getting to be a small part of my students lives by far is the best part of the job.
- A lot of my students have really hard lives. Some of them have absolutely wonderful supportive families of course. But some don't.
- I go out of my way to just love them.
- I greet them all with goofy little names like sugar and doodlebug, and I compliment them and build them up.
- I want to be a kind and safe space for them.
- They love me right back and they're just the best, even the tough kids and the behavior problems, etc.

What would make your job easier/better?

A:

- Actual curriculum would help.
- Supplies and resources.
- Having more teachers would help.
- The ones we have keep either quitting or going on maternity leave.
- Having the contract settled would help. Maybe teachers would stop pouring out of the district.

What's your favorite thing to teach?

A:

- I like teaching writing, especially now that the students have Chromebooks.
- I have them build essays part by part rather than giving them a whole essay at once.
- They get very overwhelmed by writing.
- I like having them work on figurative language and trying to incorporate it in their writing. I'll put pictures up and have them describe the picture using figurative language.
- That can be so fun and really pull poetic language out of them. Like last year I had a girl who would barely write anything describe a picture of a fish tank with the cutest little phrases like the "swishes of fishes" and comparing the orange in their fins to traffic cones. I was so proud of her.
- I also like teaching vocabulary. I've gotten better and better at it. I have pictures to illustrate different words and concepts. It really helps them, especially the English language learners.

What do you find more difficult to teach?

A:

- I'm not as good at teaching reading comprehension as I am writing, but I'm getting better at that as well. The key is Building their background knowledge first before diving into a text.
- There is no end to what they don't know or haven't been exposed to.
- Here's an example of that: a couple of years ago, we took students to a wacky house museum that had a stuffed bear in it. One of my students said you mean bears are real!? He had no idea. So, you have to set background knowledge for anything you read so that they can start making connections and inferences. If you don't even know what a bear is or that it's real how can you understand, for example, Goldilocks and the Three Bears?

What do you think kids need to succeed at school?

A:

- I think what kids need but what they lack right now is grit. It's like they don't want to work or learn or remember or retain or quest for knowledge in any way or shape.
- It's hard to fight against that.
- They sit there and just let your words flow over them like a knowledge shower and then they just dry off and go home completely unchanged.
- It's frustrating and I don't know how to change it.
- But they also need support and backing from home to try to build some desire to learn. Without that foundation it's so difficult to get anywhere.

If you had an unlimited budget to "fix" your school, what changes would you make?
A:

- More teachers.
- Curriculum and supplies!
- Heaters and air conditioners that work.
- Please, God. Somebody fix the elevator!
- If I really was going to fix it, the school would no longer be K to 8.

If you could educate/correct a few misconceptions about teaching, what would they be? In other words, what do you wish the general public (or heck, even suburban teachers) knew about your job?
A:

- I get tired of that garbage people spew about how teachers get so many vacations and the summer off. If they knew what kind of crap we put up with, they'd shut up about that.
- And I wish people knew how much teachers give for their students. Teachers are buying things and doing extra stuff and worrying about their students and on and on and on. No one really seems to understand what the job takes.

Is this a job or a calling for you? Would you move to a different district for better pay?
A:

- It must be a calling because it's a real crappy job in so many ways.
- I think about it, and actually, I did a bunch of interviewing last summer. But part of me is torn. I feel like the students I have need me in a way that suburban students wouldn't. Do you know what I mean?

Me: Yes. There will always be students who need you, regardless of your situation. But there's also always the feeling that you were carefully placed in that position for a reason to reach one or two specific kids at a crisis time in their lives.

What challenges do your students face?
A:
- Mine are like food insecure.
- A lot of my students do a lot of work around their house like raising other siblings because their parents are working multiple jobs or whatever. So, that's a challenge.

Quick definition: Food insecurity means the household as a whole lacks the ability for all members to get daily adequate food. **Me:** I'm sure some of mine are food insecure, but it's less common in suburban districts. Most of my students are hopeless phone addicts. Different world, different problem. Still, a need students have.

Takeaways:
- Urban students are often food insecure. (Well, more often than suburban students.)
- Teachers put a lot of extra into the job (time, money, energy, etc.)
- There seems to be a shortage of grit in the current batch of students. (That's true for both urban and suburban students.)

Chapter 26:
Episode 146 – Special Guest: Kendra Griffin – College Writing and Literature Professor Part 1

Introduction:

Dear Reader,

Some people relish the anonymity, and others, don't need it.

Our current guest, Kendra Griffin, falls into the latter category.

~Ann

What kind of school did you attend? Did you enjoy school?

Kendra Griffin: Despite being raised by my highly educated mother, a teacher, and my well-read father, a policeman, I lost confidence in myself as a student once I entered high school.

My troubled homelife, due to the death of my mother and ensuing alcoholism of my father, seeped into my studies.

I didn't see myself as bright any longer, though I still loved reading and writing creatively.

I, luckily, had the good sense to attend community college. From there I regained my confidence, transferred to a S.U.N.Y (State University of New York) college, and found my place, so to speak. There, I realized the power of education to transform lives and psyches.

I'm grateful for my struggle with academia as it makes me better able to relate to my students and their own less-than-perfect educational experiences before they land in my classroom.

Me: You're the second person in a row to confirm that point, though from the opposite perspective.

The last guest, A, said she picked up on school things easily, which makes relating to her students' struggles a challenge at times.

You're saying you struggled, and in a way, that's good because you can connect better and empathize with your students' struggles.

What kind of training did you do for your job?
Kendra Griffin: I hold a MA (Master's of Arts) in Literature, have taken several grad-level education classes, and recently used the Covid lockdown to acquire an online TESOL certificate.

I take every scrap of professional development my college offers, including remote and online teaching andragogy.

Me: Definitions: (Yup, I Googled them both, though I had heard of the first.)
- TESOL = Teaching English to Speakers of Other Languages
- Andragogy (<-- never seen this word in my life) = super-duper, fancy way of saying adult education

Did you always know what you wanted to do? How old were you when that realization hit? In other words, how did you end up with the job you have/are going to talk about?

Kendra Griffin: I tried to avoid becoming a teacher, both because I watched my mother be helplessly overworked and because I doubted my ability to ever be as amazing at it as she was.

But my natural inclination to tutor and mentor others kept shunting me toward this job.

I carry my insecurity with me into every classroom, but it's tempered by a deep faith in the process of teaching and learning overall.

Once I begin teaching, I forget to be nervous until the next class period.

Me: Never thought I'd become a teacher, but I didn't fight it too hard.

What other jobs did you hold before this?

Kendra Griffin:
- Waitress
- Bartender
- Chambermaid
- Office assistant
- Cashier
- Retail clerk
- Tutor
- Proofreader
- Market researcher
- Editor

Me: That's quite the list. Also, sounds like a tough list.

Please describe your job. What do you do?

Kendra Griffin: I'm a college composition, creative writing, and literature professor.

I also mentor colleagues, advise our creative writing club, and participate in numerous committees, mostly of the rabble-rousing variety.

When working with students, I spend less time teaching and more time troubleshooting their tech questions or trying to help them find resources to learn the basic skills needed to even take my classes, which is extremely disheartening.

Is this your dream job?

Kendra Griffin: It was, until I began teaching less than answering emails or defending my grades to stressed-out students who are unprepared for my classes.

Once our college dropped entrance assessments, I began to lose my love for the job.

I now use this analogy: I used to think of myself as a general practitioner, helping patients thrive.

Now I'm an oncologist, always giving bad news and offering crummy options. (I.e., "Because your average is under 50%, I urge you to meet with an advisor before the Withdraw deadline.")

Me: That's a sad, yet awesome analogy.

What equipment/stuff do you need to do your job?

Kendra Griffin: Little, but the extent to which I am expected to troubleshoot our college's tech issues is overwhelming.

Yet if I don't, the students suffer.

If you didn't need to work for the money, would you still hold the same job?

Kendra Griffin: No. I know this because I recently resigned from my tenured position to go part-time and write more.

However, I will always teach. It's magical.

Takeaways:

- Tech troubles can hinder learning.
- Kendra has had a LOT of jobs.
- Teaching is magical.
- Entrance exams are good things.
- Shared struggles can help one empathize with another.

Chapter 27:
Episode 147: Special Guest: Kendra Griffin – College Writing and Literature Professor Part 2

Introduction:

Dear Reader,

This round we get into more of the advice part of the interview. Kendra has some deep wisdom to share with us.

~Ann

What advice do you have for those considering your career? (Any training, tips, hints, tricks?)

Kendra Griffin:

- Establish reasonable boundaries for yourself early on. Don't let the higher-ups convince you that you're valuable or special because of how much you devote to your job. You *are* valuable and special, and your students are lucky to have you. But your institution will exploit you shamelessly if you cannot value your time and well-being.

- Look to trusted mentors and ask how they have established meaningful boundaries.
- Your colleagues are amazing. Forget competition. Focus on solidarity. Remember that if you let yourself be exploited, you send a message to your institution that justifies their exploitation of everyone around you.

Me: That's a very interesting point. Never really thought of it that way, though I am the sort to stay late to grade in my classroom.
I also answer emails at all hours of the day and night, which has the potential to set an odd precedent.

Kendra Griffin:
- Keep your ego in check.
- Good teaching relies on listening, on presence, and on setting your ego aside in the classroom.

What life lessons has your job taught you?
Kendra Griffin:
- Students are not unmotivated, for the most part. They simply have not learned to trust that accountability for their own education is within their grasp.
- Also, some people have never been truly listened to, and the first time that they realize you take them seriously as a student—take seriously the contents inside their head— that's magical.
- Don't forget to keep doing that and to keep letting them know you're doing that.

Me: I like your last point.

There are times I will do a lot for my students but not tell them, and then, I wonder why they don't really appreciate the efforts.

Are you close with your family?
Kendra Griffin: My closest family is comprised of friends/found

family, and I don't take this term lightly.

Family means sticking around when things are hard. (I'm not advocating that any of us endure toxic dynamics, however).

My close biological family members all passed young. Still, my relationship with them evolves as I evolve.

I unabashedly offer that they are with me every day, and I'm still learning from them. And I believe, they also learn from me.

Me: Found family still counts.

What do you do for fun?
Kendra Griffin:
- Write, write, write.
- Also, I play dorky Lovecraft cooperative boardgames with my younger friends. They forgive me for not being cool.

Would you survive in an apocalypse? Why or why not?
Kendra Griffin: I would very likely be eaten quickly because I don't want to live in a world that is any unkinder than it already is. I also would never be able to "eat the dog." Ironically though, I have published several young adult apocalyptic novels that are surprisingly light-hearted. I suspect that having survived some emotionally apocalyptic events gave me a good sense of humor.

Life is a tragicomedy.

Me: I generally do not like mashed words, but this one works.

What animal do you most relate to?
Kendra Griffin: Dogs. Paws down, dogs.

See my above note.

I would probably give my last scrap of food to my dog.

I say that not because I imagine myself as selfless but because I know, as I've pointed out here, what makes life worth living.

Sometimes, I go to shelters and reassure the animals they will all be okay and find good homes. I very much hope that is true.

If you could convey just one life lesson to someone, what would it be?

Kendra Griffin: Love yourself, and don't just assume you know what that phrase means.

Think it through, then do it with all your heart.

And if you do figure it out, let me know how you managed that feat.

Just because I'm giving you this advice doesn't mean I've mastered it yet.

Takeaways:
- Love yourself.
- Dogs are awesome.
- Some students just need someone to really listen to them and help them believe their educational goals are within their grasp.
- Establishing boundaries is important, especially in the education business.

Chapter 28:
Episode 148 – Open Letter to Non-Renewed Teachers

Introduction:
Dear Reader,

This is the time of year when school boards start finalizing their budgets for the new year and determining who they will invite back.

I've probably mentioned it before, but teaching is an oddball profession where the contracts are renewed annually.

In public school districts, you can eventually get tenure, which then affords you some additional job security (in some cases probably too much). This isn't about that debate.

Since I've talked about a lot of stuff, I'm honestly not sure if this particular topic has come up in this way. I'll likely do a prayer version of this topic soon because that's a slightly different focus. Here, I want to discuss the topic in an informative way because I'm not sure how many people not in the business know what happens.

Disclaimer and clarification: There are likely more reasons than I can list here.

Quick definitions first for orientation purposes:

- Fired – Teacher is removed from their position effective immediately because they did something grievous enough to warrant that. (This looks bad for everybody, so most districts don't do it on a whim.)
- Forced resignation – Teacher is given the option to resign, usually effective immediately. This is in lieu of being fired. Sometimes, there's the threat of legal action, but whether that has teeth or not is hard to say.
- Non-Renewal – Teacher is informed that they will not have a job next year but will finish out the current school year. (This is what I want to talk about.)
- Voluntary Resignation – Teacher says (internally or externally) "heck with this" and leaves the teaching position, likely also the profession. Generally, you need to give 60 days notice to the district so they can find an adequate replacement.
- Giving 60 days notice – Would likely happen if the teacher wants to leave for a new position.
- Not giving 60 days notice – If the teacher doesn't intend to ever continue being a teacher, they wouldn't need to stay in the school's good graces.

~Ann

Dear Non-Renewed Teachers,

First, I'm sorry you're in this position. I know it can be shocking, jarring, emotionally disturbing, and probably a dozen other things I'm not thinking of right now.

Second, I've been there quite a few times. Three, in fact.

Some people get their first job at a school and spend a 35+ year career at the same place. It takes others of us a few districts before we find our forever ones.

The person whose post reminded me to write this letter went with the anonymous option, so I truly don't know who you are or your exact situation. This person sounded hurt and confused as to why this would be happening. (No bad observations. A few parent interactions they thought ended okay.)

The options:
- It's you.
- It's them.
- It's something else.

Is it you or is it them or is it something else?
Honestly, this answer can go any which way.

As others suggested on the thread I'm thinking about, it could just be internal politics. We like to think that nepotism, favoritism, and other nasty little -isms won't factor in, but they do.

(This person mentioned that one parent she had a run in with has a brother on the board, so this is likely an open-shut case of internal backdoor deals biting her.)

The top two options can be seen as different sides of the same coin. The point is that you aren't the right teacher for that position. Many times, it's their (the district's) loss. Occasionally, it's you need the time to grow into or find yourself as a teacher.

Sometimes, it's just the wrong fit.

After my first year of teaching, I was ready to quit the profession altogether. Was working in a public school teaching one subject under a brand new supervisor who had just come off a career as a stellar teacher of that subject. Basically, he didn't know what he was doing. I didn't know what I was doing. The kids were a mix of sweet, lovely people and entitled brats and they were freshmen to book. That basically means, they didn't know what they were doing.

That lovely mix led to me being non-renewed. The ultimate reason was never given, but I'm going to file it under *a bit of everything*. I ended up teaching a different science subject at a private Christian high school after that first year from Hades. (Quick reminder, most first-year of teaching experiences are awful in many ways.)

Four years later, their enrollment took a dive, and I was non-renewed again. This particular reason doesn't often come up in public schools because their funding is steadier. Private schools rely on tuition and donations to make it, so when economic downturns hit, families often cut out the major expense of tuition and send their kids to public schools. Thus, the private school ends up with a shortfall in their budget for the upcoming school term. Cuts got to happen somewhere.

I got certified to teach the subject I was teaching at the private school.

(Had to go back to college for a semester to do that.)

Next up, got a public school position covering the new subject. Stayed there about 2.5 years before being non-renewed yet again. That time, I think I just wasn't the dream team member this district had imagined. Or the supervisor wanted to do something to justify her existence. Dunno. For whatever reason, it happened. I scrounged around for a new job, and landed in my current position. This is year 8 or so at the "new" school. (And now I feel old for admitting that.)

A few points:
- Try not to be discouraged. Non-renewal is a district's nod that you're trusted enough to finish a school term.

- It can royally stink. Nobody likes being told they're "not good enough" for whatever.

- It can be a blessing in disguise. The private school I was working at paid legitimately less than half of what I can make in a public school. But, given my personality, I'm not sure I would have voluntarily left.

- It's very easy to let those negative emotions steamroll you. (Trust me, I cried a lot the first time it happened before I grew into the knowledge that it may or may not be about me.)

- There is always another school to teach at. People come and go from districts for many reasons. (Reaching retirement, moving out of state, having kids and wanting to focus on parenting for a few years, etc.)

- There will always be more students who need you, regardless of location.

- If you choose to stick with the profession, it does get better (or you get better coping mechanisms.)

- It's not a failing to leave the profession altogether. There are a lot of jobs in the world. Each comes with its own brand of stress. If this isn't the kind of stress you want or need in your life, file the good memories away and move on without regret.

You need to do what's right for you.

If that's entering the great job hunt for another teaching position, go for it. If that's hanging up the teaching spurs forever, go for it. The main point is that if you want to be a teacher, nobody can permanently take it from you.

~Ann

Takeaways:

- Non-renewal is not a comfortable thing, but it's also not the end of the world. (Might seem like it for a time.)
- There's nothing wrong with not wanting to continue in the profession.
- There will always be another teaching job out there for you if you want it.

Chapter 29:
Episode 149 – Special Guest Anonymous Teacher Speaks about Being the Supervisor's Pet Project

Introduction:

Dear Ann,

I've heard horror stories of course, but until this year, I had avoided being on the supervisor's radar.

Trust me. You do not want to be on the supervisor's radar. It's not a fun place to be.

Within the past month or two, I've been in my supervisor's office at least 4 times. Upon further reflection, only two instances were for this annoying stuff.

One time, she got called in by a guidance counselor. Honestly, that's on the guidance counselor. I have no idea why the counselor decided to go to the supervisor to ask me a question. That's just dumb. The supervisor didn't know the answer and had to ask me because it pertained to my class. If the dumb counselor had just come to me, I could have clarified it right away. (The issue was something silly like a kid being able to chew gum in a class normally not allowed to do so.)

Once, I think I was recapping something that had happened pertaining to one of my students. That was with a different supervisor and not a problem. He just wanted to keep me informed about what happened with a different situation.

I'm a fully tenured teacher who has been in this district for more than seven years. I get observed twice. Those are done and went fine.

So, what the heck is this horse poopy?

My supervisor occasionally comes around to classes and pops in for a few minutes to take pictures for the school's social media accounts. That's fine.

She's also started to come around to observe for an additional half hour. Then, she calls a meeting. (She sends an email that says, "Do you have time to meet?") She happened to do this on my busiest day. Mind you, this woman has access to my schedule and doesn't really check her email sometimes.

That means, it's hard to schedule a meeting.

After teaching several classes and labs in a row, I eat my lunch and head over to see when we can meet. And she's on the phone. So, I wait. And wait. And wait.

And wait some more.

Finally, a few minutes into the next period, she gets off the phone long enough for me to claim the meeting.

Her major critiques were as follows:
- What I'd called a Do Now is really an activity.

- My lower-level students aren't great with following directions like write down the questions, so I should give them lined paper with the questions typed for them.
- I should demand their attention before trying to give directions. (In some classes, I might die of old age before they voluntarily quiet down.)

At one point in the meeting, I asked where this was coming from. (Are there student complaints? Parent complaints?) As usual, she dodged the question.

On the one hand, I'm grateful that she didn't really have anything to complain about. On the other hand, I'm annoyed that I've had to waste an hour of my life for nothing.

I did let her know that it felt like being singled out. She assured me she was doing this to multiple people. While misery loves company, not sure I'm pleased with the idea of her bothering my colleagues either.

Calling for a meeting is needlessly stressful, and it gives off the message that you don't trust your people. It also disrupts the learning environment. The kids think the supervisor is there babysitting them. I just want to tell them they don't have to worry, she's there to bother me, not them.

Kind of makes you feel like a 5-year-old called to the principal's office.

Not sure there's much you can do, but thanks for letting me share my frustrations.

~Anonymous Teacher

Dear Anonymous Teacher,

I'm sorry you're in this situation. That indeed sounds frustrating. I call this phenomenon being the supervisor's pet project.

You're welcome to share your frustrations at any time. That's why this project exists. I'm not sure if any supervisors will ever read this, but I happen to have been in a similar situation recently, so I can at least tell you what some of my friends said.

- Sorry, this is happening to you.
- Hopefully, she'll get sidetracked and move onto something new sometime soon.
- She'll probably die down once she has summative reports to occupy her attention. Now, she has two much free time, and, from her mouth, she visited 7 classes today. (She's really making the rounds.)
- This is micromanaging.

A bored supervisor is a dangerous thing.

Another wise colleague once shared that supervisors need to cover their butts. (Justify their existence.) When that happens, they get busy bothering people.

I agree that meetings with supervisors can be stressful.

You seem to have a good perspective, and it sounds like the situation will right itself in time.

One of the most annoying aspects of education is that good is never good enough in the eyes of the higher-ups. One should always strive to improve and be better next year.

On a philosophical level, I see the merit of seeking to improve, but I'm also of the opinion that there's not enough celebration of what's going right.

I also tend to flip this around. One of my students called me the supervisor of the class today. That made me laugh. But there's a grain of truth in there. Because I know how much it stinks to be singled out like this, I'll try to be mindful of that when it comes to pulling students aside to talk about one thing or another. (Meetings with any authority figure can be stressful. Try to keep things casual and friendly.)

Take heart in the fact that your supervisor's comments (suggestions?) are not difficult, big-ticket items.

Seek the support of your teacher friends (and mine). Hopefully, the supervisor will move on sooner rather than later.

~Ann

Takeaways:
- Meetings with authority figures can be stressful.
- Frustrating situations usually have an expiration date.
- Micromanaging can happen in almost any profession.

Chapter 30:
Episode 150 – Special Guest: Anonymous Christian Teacher – I Need Advice

Introduction:

This is my response to something that was posted anonymously in a Facebook Group.

I didn't stylize it as a letter, but I wanted to talk about it because it's a situation that's common enough.

Spoiler: This is going to be about the importance of communication.

The situation:
Background:

- The person was asking for advice.
- The teacher is team leader for a second-grade class.
- The Lead Teacher has a colleague who's hard to work with.

Background issues:

The person in question ...

- Misses meetings.
- Doesn't check email.
- Doesn't do grades on time.
- Doesn't take correction or instruction well.

What happened:
- One incident pushed the Lead Teacher to say something. That sort of made the Errant Teacher defensive.
- Lead Teacher sort of laid down the law because she'd had enough.
- Lead Teacher explained via email that the breakdown in communication is hurting the team as a whole.
- Unrelated, administration pulled the Errant Teacher aside and forced her to sit down and finish her grades. (Errant teacher blames the lead teacher for this even though the timing was a coincidence.)
- I think Lead Teacher was feeling guilty.

Sample responses and advice: (There were more.)
- Rest.
- Will pray.
- Proud of you!
- Document everything.
- Keep admin in the loop.
- Christian doesn't mean doormat.
- Boundaries don't make you a bad guy.
- Advocate for your team and yourself. This is good.
- Jesus flipped tables. Sometimes you need to be blunt.
- People need to do their jobs. You shouldn't feel bad about it.
- Doesn't sound like you were harsh about it. It just needed saying.

My response:

I had asked if the teacher's new because a lot of the complaints sound like stuff someone would quickly learn to fix if they wanted their year to run smoothly.

Don't even know where this teaching team is located but my school term is midway into the third quarter and my state tends to be later than most of the rest of the country. Point is, it's late in the year.

I like to think I'm organized, but teaching at the high school level has different needs than elementary.

The complaints seem like a bad combination.

Me double-checking that my colleagues couldn't say the same about me.

- I do grades weekly.
- I check email obsessively.
- I don't think I could bring myself to miss meetings, though I will openly complain to any friendly ear in range.
- Have been in the situation where admin is all up in one's grill, and it's annoying as heck.

Some of the differences:

Elementary:

- Elementary teachers are with the kids way longer than high school teachers. They take them around to specials at varying points of the day, but otherwise, it's one teacher and a set amount of kiddos.
- Elementary teachers tend to work in teams.
- Elementary teachers usually get to teach the kids more basic skills like sharing, tying one's shoes, not wrestling in the middle of class, not walloping each other for fun, etc.

High School:
- Some high school teachers work in teams, but they usually only consist of two people: a special education teacher and a general education teacher.
- High school kids take themselves around to various teachers throughout the day.
- High school teachers specialize in one subject.
- High school teachers do occasionally have to get the kids to stop wrestling in class. (I might have had to do that today. I definitely had to do that today.)

Both:
- Society seems to want both teacher types to teach kids phone etiquette. (It feels like a losing battle.)

Takeaways:
- Correcting people's behavior is never easy. (They get defensive. It usually ends with an altercation. Even justified altercations take a toll on everybody.)
- Confrontation of any sort can be difficult. A large set of the population (me raising my hand) will go way out of their way to avoid any sort of confrontation.
- Communication is paramount to success. If there's a breakdown in communication, it can be difficult to get back into the groove of things.

Chapter 31:
Episode 151 – Special Guest Anonymous Teacher's Parent Report, PSA, and Rant Part 1

Introduction:

Dear Reader,

Going to have to break this up. It contains a lot of great information that deserves to be pondered in greater detail than I can do if I lump it all as one.

~Ann

Dear Ann,

Somebody told me this was a safe space to be honest about the frustrations involved in teaching.

I hope you don't mind if I ramble. I have some stories to tell you. Maybe you'll have advice for me, maybe you won't, but as my mother used to say, better out than in.

Ann: I'd like to think it's exactly what you've described, and I do love stories.

Anonymous Teacher: I'll start by saying most parents are lovely. I hardly ever hear from them. This is the way it ought to be, unless I'm reaching out to them to keep them up to date or letting them know their kid owes me work.

Other people, I don't hear from because they go straight over my head to the supervisor and school principal.

First, let me say that I'm a tenured high school science teacher, and I work with a co-teacher for one of the courses I teach this year. Thank goodness because I can't imagine the hell this would put me through if I was new to the business.

So, the saga begins before the school year. This kid had a reputation coming up of having a crazy mother. Never a good thing, but also something I have zero control over.

Okay, so the kid gets a B the first two marking periods and is currently pulling a C for the third marking period.

Ann: Aside.

A C is average, but some people cannot abide them.

Anonymous Teacher: The mother calls a meeting with special services, me, my co-teacher, and my boss.

During the course of the hour-long meeting, she's explaining how useless her kid is at home (poor "executive functioning skills"). The special services people and the mother start harping on meeting the kid regularly after school (but it can't be on a rotating schedule, has to be a fixed day, let's aim for 10 minutes.)

I believe I said, "it's pointless." While I was referring to a ten-minute meeting, the mother misinterpreted the statement and walked out of the meeting. I'd looked down to put a reminder in my phone about the twice-a-week meetings, and when I looked up, poof, she was gone. (Too bad she didn't stay gone.)

Ann: Misunderstandings happen. That's why communication is a very important thing.

Anonymous Teacher: Anyway, that got me yelled at by my boss, which is just dandy.

How is it my fault the lady can't handle stuff like an adult? You know, ask "What do you mean by that?" wherein she could get an immediate explanation.

The answer being that ten minutes isn't enough time.

She'd just spent a half-hour explaining how hard it is to work with her kid. What makes special services or the mother think a ten-minute meeting twice a week is going to fix the kid in my class?

A ten-minute meeting with an advanced placement kid would be useless unless it's a very quick question.

Once the special services people and my boss coaxed the lady back into the room, we eventually got around to hashing out a plan to help her kid do better. This included daily review questions, twice-a-week meetings for about a half-hour, and my co-teacher taking notes for him like a freakin' secretary.

(Note taking is actually very common on IEPs (Individualized Education Plan). I get the point of them, but some veer into the ridiculous. This kid's is a small novel. I won't give you specifics, but the modifications span a few pages.)

A colleague of mine told me he had a kid once upon a time whose IEP said that he couldn't put in an assignment grade of missing. It had to say incomplete because missing made the kid feel bad. (This is what I mean by ridiculous. Literally, that's the same thing in the grade book. My incompletes show up in bright colors, but that's a setting on my end.)

After the ill-fated meeting, I haven't had any more contact with the woman, but she's been all up in my boss's and her boss's grill. Co-teacher too. Apparently, she was still upset after the meeting, even after having the infamous this is pointless statement explained to her.

Holding a grudge much?

Ann: I see this goes on for quite a bit more. I'm going to have to cut it off here so I can respond to the first half and give the readers time to process the first section of your saga.

Random responses:

- First, that does sound frustrating.
- It's a natural human tendency to hold grudges, but it's certainly not one of our finer traits. I can also see how one could misinterpret the statement, but I agree with you that the lady seems to have overreacted.
- Ten-minute meetings do seem short.
- For all its faults, the tenure system does provide some protection from cases like this parent. Districts do some shady stuff, and I wouldn't put it past them to sacrifice a newbie teacher to appease a parent.

Takeaways:

- Communication is very important.
- Talking is important.
- Talking is not possible if one storms out of a meeting.
- Assume the best.
- Ask for clarification if something seems off to you.

Chapter 32:
Episode 152 – Special Guest Anonymous Teacher's Parent Report, PSA, and Rant Part 2

Introduction:

Dear Reader,

Welcome back.

Anonymous Teacher had a whole lot more to say, so I'll let her get to it.

(We'll get to the Public Service Announcement today. Sorry for the delay.)

~Ann

Anonymous Teacher: I think there's other stuff going on with students bothering this kid. So, now the mother is coming in with a lawyer. That part has nothing to do with me, but she's also harping on my class because the kid has some low scores.

Ann: Kids can be cruel. Sadly, bullying too has become a buzzword.

The kids like to throw it around and accuse each other of being bullies.

Anonymous Teacher: Here's the thing. Kid has low scores because he didn't hand in large pieces of a project or one of the labs.

No work. No grade.

As explained to the parents in the beginning of the year and several times throughout, a zero goes in to remind students to make up their work.

When we get work, magically, grades show up in the grading program.

This could have been cleared up with a quick conversation or an email to me, but why talk to the people who can fix your problems when you can bother their boss and their boss's boss?

My co-teacher asked me to not put in grades until we get the kid to do the work. His grade is a low B without the 0's. I'll do it for my co-teacher, but the mother has effectively burnt any good will I ever had toward her to a crisp.

Did the kid do the work? Yes, he did at least part in one of the after-school meetings. But he still didn't hand it in. Can't grade what I don't have. I asked him about the project piece that was missing and got a promise to turn something in later. Later came and went and nada.

Why is this even a conversation with special services, the co-teacher, and such? Lady, tell your kid to hand in the dang work.

Ann: Sounds reasonable.

Maybe grade the kid based on the memory of what he did in your presence? Did he do a lot in your presence?

Anonymous Teacher:
I guess this is my Public Service Announcement.

Don't be this parent.

Nothing good comes of being the one people dread to deal with. (I know some people relish the role.) Sure, you get your way, but evaluate if it's doing you, your stress levels, and your kid any favors in the long run. You've effectively poisoned the water around your kid, making them a pariah.

Love your kid. Certainly.

Teach them right from wrong. Definitely.

Fight their battles when they're too young to do so themselves. Maybe. 16 is not too young. By this point in life, one should be able to accept responsibility for not turning in work, especially if you have a free pass to hand things in whenever you feel like it.

Ann: All great points. Thanks for sharing. Do you have any closing thoughts?

Anonymous Teacher: I feel like the system is failing because we let it happen.

It's a vicious cycle.

Kid doesn't do something or can't do something for one reason or another. We write an IEP to help them reach their full potential. (In theory, this is good.) Something falls through because the kid doesn't hold up their end of the bargain (do the work).

Crazy Parent comes charging in yelling at everybody and anybody. Special Services, teachers, people who generally don't like being yelled at, bend over backwards to appease Crazy Parent.

Crazy Parent learns yelling gets results. Next time anybody sneezes wrong, CP defaults to yelling and threats.

I can see the cycle, but I don't know how to break it. Very few people relish confrontation.

Nobody wants to stand up to combative parents. (Let's be honest, it's usually the mother.) This is a problem because then the kids wind up in classes they're not really cut out for. You can't have it both ways. Either your kid is a genius and can hack it in a harder class, or they need additional supports and should be in an appropriately leveled course.

The kid would have an easier time and be less stressed, but nobody's willing to tell these people the truth because there's zero gain. People with this attitude interpret any sort of this brand of truth as a direct attack against their kid.

Ann:
Agreed. I think sometimes people forget that teachers are on the side of doing what's best for the kids.

Speaking of leveling ...

Skiing analogy:
It would be highly irresponsible to throw a beginner skier onto a black diamond slope. They're not ready for it. People can enjoy skiing on the intermediate slopes or the bunny hills, but if you throw them onto slopes they're not ready for, they will struggle.

Anonymous Teacher: By the time it comes to hand the kid off to the next grade's teacher, the current year teacher is just happy to be done with them. That's kind of sad.

Equity is a big buzzword in education. There's a lovely picture of kids watching a ball game from a fence. One just watches because he's tall enough to see over the fence. Another needs a box to stand on because they're short.

The concept is lovely.

The reality is messier.

At what point do you draw the line? In high school, classes are leveled so all kids can get the most out of the class in terms of pacing, structure, and supports.

Ann: This makes sense. I tend to expect more out of the college-bound groups than I do the lower level. I think the problem kicks in because kids are cruel and have no qualms about equating a lower level with special education classes and equating that with being dumb.

Special thanks to Anonymous Teacher for sharing her thoughts with us. (She gave her name. I'm choosing to make it anonymous because not every thought in the last two Chapters will be a popular one.)

Takeaways:
- Don't be the nuisance parent people dread to deal with.
- Love your kids, but also, be realistic about their capabilities.
- A lower-level class doesn't mean your kid is dumb. It means, the subject may not be their passion, and/or their current skill-level in the course isn't up to the rigors of a really fast-paced survey of the course. (That's okay. I'm definitely not passionate about all subjects. That's a part of life.)
- If high level math and science isn't their thing, don't push them to be that. There are plenty of opportunities in the world.
- Nobody who isn't a silly, immature child is going to give two figs about what level science class your kid is in.
- Be kind.

- There's probably a time and place for bringing a lawyer, but that tends to make things more contentious.
- Teachers are generally on your kid's side.

Chapter 33:
Episode 153 – Easter (Spring Break) Morale Booster Part 1 - Basics

Introduction:

Dear Reader,

Figured I should talk about this one while it's fresh in my mind.

It wasn't as popular as the Christmas one, but that could be a trick of the timing. A lot of people *meant to sign up* and just didn't.

It's fine. Lots of leftover candy to go around. (I saved some of the good stuff for me. It helps that I typically only buy stuff I'll eat.)

The 30-some people who did sign up appreciated it.

I enjoy being able to invite people back to grab a second or third set of candy anyway.

~Ann

How does the Easter/Spring Break version differ from the Christmas one?

- The Christmas packages are wrapped, so the setup is a bit longer.
- The mechanics differ. In the Christmas one, the slips of paper declaring a special prize go into certain packages, so if someone doesn't get a special prize, they just don't have a slip of paper.

Mechanics of the Easter/Spring Break edition:

- Every package gets a slip of paper with a number and a brief description. (I.e. 1 SPK; chocolate pack. That stands for Sour Patch Kids and means that the rest of the candy in the pack could have chocolate things.)
- This year, we put the "big" prizes in the bags where possible. I used the cheap plastic sandwich bags that fold over because they're the most flexible. They let things like a package of gummy bears be crammed inside. (Tight fit, but it works.)
- Every slip of paper in a package has a twin that will go into an egg.
- The people who sign up pick an egg, open it, and take a paper. (I let them check all the slips in the egg, but you could totally just say it has to be a blind draw or have more eggs that only get 1 slip of paper each. Because I get lazy and keep buying eggs, this will theoretically be possible someday.)

How to run something like this:

- Step 1: Buy candy. To run it with special prizes, you need to buy normal fun-sized candy as well as the movie theater boxes and other specials.
- Step 2: Catalogue the special prizes.

- Step 3: Sort candy. (Note: This could be a problem if you have a dog, ornery cats, kids, or both because there will be candy on the floor for a while. I guess you could do it on a dining room or kitchen table, but that might not be enough room. Wherever you do the sorting, make sure it has plenty of room for the 60-ish piles of candy.
- Step 4: Bag the candy and add the slips to the bag and an egg. (I made orange my non-chocolate packs because the person who doesn't eat chocolate loves that color. You may wish to have some non-chocolate/low allergens packages available.)
- Step 5: Write your invitation letter and Google doc if you want to run signups. (They help because then if someone doesn't come down, I deliver it to their mailbox.)

Notes:

- I consistently end up with about 65 to 70 packages, but you can scale down a little by buying less candy.
- You can also run this any time of the year, but it can be helpful to have a cause for celebration like Spring Break or the Christmas/Winter break.

Sample Email:

Hi,

I feel late with this. I don't think I'm late with this, but anyways, sign up (insert appropriate hyperlink) if you want goodies.

Come by Room (insert yours here) on (whichever day you want to run this) to pick an egg and pick 1 slip of paper out of that egg. Then, you and the helper (maybe me, maybe an innocent teacher conscripted to help) will get to search the candy bags for the right prizes.

Beautiful chaos ensues, I'm sure.

Note: Not going to post the Google doc because it's almost identical to the Christmas published in Chapter 139.

Random points:
- A little kindness goes a long way.
- Adults like candy too.
- Stick with a budget if money is tight.
- Gauge your audience. I get lottery tickets because I work in a public school. If you work in a school with religious affiliation, you may or may not want to include something that's a wee bit of gambling.
- Go with what you're passionate about (within reason!). By that, I mean, if candy's not your thing but baking is, you could make the base prize cookies or brownies. In that case, I'd go with taping the numbered slips to the outside of the bag. The thought of baking something puts an I-suck-lemons-for-a-living expression on my face, so I just buy loads of candy from a store. The baking option is likely cheaper in the long run.
- Things are getting more expensive, so if you're worried about cost, you'll have to be a little more careful than my grab-whatever-strikes-your-fancy approach.
- I'll deep-dive into the costs later, both time and money.
- It's not really about what the candy is, though there are definitely better and gross-er candies.
- It's fun to win. People can buy their own candy for the most part, but it's nicer when someone else does the buying.
- I run stuff like this a few times a year.

Takeaways:
- Candy is a good way to cheer people.
- (Teachers also need love and respect too, but a small treat is nice.)
- This can be adapted for almost any office.

Chapter 34:
Episode 154 – Easter (Spring Break) Morale Booster Part 2 – Cost Breakdown

Introduction:
Dear Reader,

Costs are on the rise.

If you run something like this a few months from now, the cost could be completely different.

If you happen to catch an awesome candy sale, all the better. Sometimes, you can stalk the stores the day after a holiday for some quality sales, but that's certainly not a guarantee.

The list here may not include everything because I also impulse buy random candy during other shopping trips. (I also might be having trouble reading the cryptic notes on the receipt.)

~Ann

Costs of special prizes:

- M&M minis milk chocolate $2.29.
- Twix Caramel Bar $1.29. (I also might have just eaten this and not included it in the fun thing.)
- Tic Tac coca cola $1.49. (My friend said they looked gross. I'm intrigued. Might have to buy them again sometime. She's probably right.)
- Werther's caramel hard candies $3.19.
- M&Ms mystery mix $4.29.
- ShopRite orange slices $1.49.
- Airheads extreme rainbow $1.99.
- Haribo Sour streamers $2.39.
- ShopRite fruit slices $1.49.
- Sour Patch Kids Watermelon $1.29.
- Sour Patch Kids Tropical $1.29.
- Nerds rope Easter $1.00. Got two = $2.00.
- Reeses Peanut butter eggs $4.99. (There were 6 in here, so this became six prizes.)
- Junior Mints $1.50.
- Reeses Peanut butter something else $3.89.
- Cadbury Crème eggs $3.89. (I think there were 4 in the package.)
- Sour Bright Crawler egg $4.49.
- Swedish fish red $1.29.
- Sour Patch Kids $1.29.
- Kit Kat Easter packaging $4.99.
- ShopRite Bowl and Basket dark chocolate bar 72% $1.89.
- ShopRite milk chocolate bar $1.89.
- ShopRite pretzel and toffee bar $1.89.
- Cadbury fruit and nut bar $2.39. (I got two, but I definitely just ate the other.)
- $10 of small lottery tickets.

- Two $10 gift cards. (I usually stock Dunkin, Starbucks, and Panera.)
- Estimated cost for the prizes: $87.59. (I'm not including taxes this time because that will vary by state or country.)

Cost of the regular fill-the-bag candies:
- Dum Dum Bunny pops $3.19.
- Hershey's milk chocolate eggs $4.29. Got two of these. $8.58.
- Reeses Peanut butter minicups $4.29. Got two = $8.58.
- Sour Punch ministraws $3.49.
- ShopRite peppermint starlight (mints) $1.49.
- Tootsie Roll mix $6.79.
- Starburst red mix $4.99.
- Lindt Milk chocolate mix $5.19.
- Hersey's Peppermint Patties and assorted chocolates $13.69.
- Something Fun Times mix (assorted candy I'm sure) $14.99.
- Estimated cost for this section: $70.98.

Other:
Sandwich bags $3.29.

Total estimated monetary cost: $87.59 (prizes) + $70.98 (base candy) + $3.29 (bags) = $161.86.

(My grocery bill for the day was about $299, but I also did my food shopping. That used to be a lot cheaper but is clocking in about $80 a week these days.

Where can you save money?
- Don't buy lottery tickets or gift cards. $30 savings.
- Don't buy "expensive prizes" unless they carry over to multiples.

- Heck, don't do a prize section, just mix the candy and assign numbers to the bags.
- Buy less of the "filler" candy. I try to get at least 5 pieces in the bags so the thing doesn't look terribly sad.
- Try an alternative like baked cookies instead.

Time estimate:

- I think the spring one is easier than the one I run around Christmas because I don't have to individually wrap the prizes. I just shove them into their respective bags and go about my merry business.
- The shopping part took about two hours. I was back and forth over that store looking for the Easter-y stuff. I ended up getting way more normal candy than specially wrapped, but that can't be helped.
- Organizing the list took about an hour. I had to go through and catalogue the prizes.
- Sorting and putting slips in took another 1-2 hours.
- My friend helped me bulk up some of the sad looking bags later with some of the random candy that didn't make it into the sorting piles the first time. That probably took another half hour.
- Estimated 4.5-5 hours of time invested. I did it in early March and ran it in late March. (The candy always comes out the millisecond beyond Valentine's Day.)

Random points and suggestions:

- Have fun with it.
- Don't stress about it.
- Do whatever is in your budget time and money-wise.
- Invite some friends to split costs and make a mini-afternoon of it.
- Some people will want to donate to the cause. You can let that happen if you'd like to recoup some of the money part,

but I don't. People will also volunteer candy, especially after Halloween. That too could be a way to get free candy.

- You can plan it out or wing it. Go with the flow of your personality. For some, the planning part would be sort of the fun. Others, would completely dread that.
- You don't have to have edible only prizes. You can also get small supplies like pens or pencils or fun stickers or erasers (if you're a teacher). I'm sure there are equivalents in other fields.

Takeaways:

- This can be more or less expensive. Totally up to you.
- Don't stress about fun stuff.
- Be yourself.

Chapter 35:
Episode 155 – General Opinion: I Can't Make You Come to Extra Help

Introduction:
Background and introduction:
Communication is very important.

Some people are just bad at it, or so it seems.

I have one mother telling me her son's confused and didn't know what was wrong on the quiz before he took the test.

Luckily, I had already worked with this student. He said he wasn't ready to take the test, but I'd noticed he hadn't taken the quizzes either. So, I worked with him during the first half of the period, and then gave him the quiz in the second half.

His quiz scores were average, and I took the higher grade.
He came for extra help then took the test and earned a 90%.

So, why am I hearing from his mother?
Well, his overall score at the time was low because he was missing 4 of 8 assignments in the marking period.

That never does nice things for a grade.

This parent works in a school. She should know how that works. I responded that his quiz/test scores aren't the issue. It's his <u>missing assignments</u> holding the grade down. I have pretty lenient late-work policies.

As for the *he's confused* part, I said he should come for extra help and reiterated that students are always welcome to come see their quizzes and go over them with me. (Nobody ever does that outside of class, but a few will inquire in class.)

Said something to the effect of he should make an appointment with me for extra help.

The parent said I should schedule a specific time to meet him. He needs to wait at school anyway and should be available daily.

That's where I draw a line. I can ask, but I can't force anybody to come to extra help.

A 16-year-old should be more than capable of setting up his own appointment for extra help. (Or randomly dropping by enough to eventually catch me.) I explain several times in the beginning of the year, the appointments are never formal, they're just the best way of making sure I'm there when the student's looking for me. It's as casual as "hey, can I come after school (fill in the blank with whatever day)?"

What is extra help?

- Extra help takes place outside normal school hours.
- Students can make up work.
- Ask questions.
- Review lessons.
- Get additional practice problems.
- Go over assessments.
- Prepare for assessments.

One of the first assignments has a basic list of responsibilities.

My responsibilities:
- Be available for extra help.
- Give advanced warning of assignments and due dates.
- Grade things in a timely fashion.
- Answer questions – not a mind reader

Student responsibilities:
- Seek extra help.
- Complete assignments on time.
- Make up assignments in a timely fashion.

My main point is that seeking extra help is a student responsibility.
- If a student is not invested in doing better, it won't help them.

General scheduling notes:
- Everybody has a different schedule.
- Schedules change.
- If someone has to make up stuff for me because of an absence, they likely have other things to make up as well.

I can and will ...
- Make adjustments to my schedule as needed.
- Stay after school when possible.

I might ...
- Ask the student if they're planning on coming for extra help.
- Suggest the student should come to extra help.
- Reiterate my availability.

I will not ...

- Force a student to come to extra help if they're adamantly against the idea. In the past, I've had kids at morning extra help because their parents made them come. Kid sat in my classroom for 20 minutes. Probably got zero out of the experience. Another fine way to waste time.
- Wait around at random to see if students feel like dropping by for extra help. (That would be a royal waste of my time with the level of students I have.)

Note: I have a colleague who is doing almost that—staying around in case students want to come for extra help. However, the situation is very different. These are A.P. students preparing for the exam, which is less than a week away.

Takeaways:
- Extra help can be very beneficial, but only if the student wants it. (Someone forced to go to extra help, might learn something by accident, but it will be harder than if they genuinely want the help.)
- Seeking extra help is mostly a student responsibility.

Chapter 36:
Episode 156 – The Ice Cream Lab 2023 – Cost Breakdown

Introduction:

This is a lab I do every year (except during the Covid year(s)?). I like it, but it can be pricey.

I may have already written it up, but I'm too lazy to go back and check the other 155 Chapters in this series to know for sure.

I kind of hope I did because I'd like to check the prices against last year to see if there is indeed a difference.

Quick rundown of colligative properties:

- You'd think the freezing point of something would be a steady thing, but it's not.
- The freezing point can be lowered (depressed) by putting more stuff in the liquid.
- Salt (NaCl) is soluble in water. It will break into Na^{+1} ions and Cl^{-1} ions.
- So, when you put salt onto ice, it will become even colder than normal.

Random notes:

- I bought sugar even though I may not need it. I have a LOT of sugar, but some isn't good for anything but labs and this sort of needs to be fresh each year. Some might be brand new and not even expired, but it's hard as a rock. That won't help me either because I need to get my plastic cup measuring thingy into and out of it without snapping the handle. Nobody wants plastic in their ice cream.
- I may put in slightly less sugar than the recipe calls for because it's been super sweet in the past.
- Each bag has enough for about 4 servings. There are usually some extras per class.
- This lab makes a mess. Partly because kids are messy monsters and partly because shaking bags of salt is going to get it everywhere.
- Don't think of the environmental impact of this lab. It's not pretty. There's a lot of waste.
- On a small scale, you can do this at home. During Covid, I posted a video that had a rundown of how to do the lab. One of my students ran it with her brother from supplies they had at home.
- It's essentially a free day for the students. But do remind them not to destroy your room in the process.
- I typically reserve it for after the unit, but sometimes, you just need to go with the flow of where it fits in a given year.
- The students in my district do the lab in 8th grade. At least one kid per class will bring that up.

What you need for 4 classes of 6 lab groups:
Edible consumables:

- 2 four-pound bags of white sugar – It might only be one necessary, but I always get two because you really don't want to run out mid class.

- 2 gallons of whole milk
- 4 quarts of half and half
- 4 quarts of heavy cream
- 1 vial of vanilla extract (or the fake stuff)

Other consumables:

- Salt – So. Much. Salt. I budget two containers per class. This year, I got the large kosher ones because they were on sale.
- 100 9-oz plastic cups.
- 2 containers of plastic spoons
- Minimum of 24 gallon freezer bags – I actually had enough stocked up to not have to buy them this year. (You likely need more because some occasionally break or start leaking a little.
- Minimum of 24 quart freezer bags– I actually had enough stocked up to not have to buy them this year.

Things I don't buy but still need:

- A crazy amount of paper towels.
- Ice. – We tend to get it from the sports office. They have an ice machine for the teams to fill their water jugs for games and practices.
- Students should bring gloves or old sweatshirts to class to protect their hands from the ice.

Cost breakdown:

- Sugar: $3.49 x 2 = $6.98
- Whole milk: $4.49 x 2 = $8.98
- Half and half: $3.29 x 4 = $13.16
- Heavy cream: $5.99 x 4 = $23.96
- Imitation vanilla: $1.29
- Salt: Diamond Crystal Kosher salt small container $3.99 x 4 = $15.96

- Salt: Diamond Crystal Kosher salt bigger container $4.99 x 4 = $19.96
- Hefty 50 count party cups: $3.99 x 2 = $7.98
- Plastic spoons: $2.29 x 2 = $4.58
- Gallon freezer bags: BJ's (Costco's alternative) has them at 152-count for $18.99. I'm going to use that price because I tend to get them on sale throughout the year. (I got some at $0.99 once upon a time, but that was like the 15-count package. I believe they're $1.99 on sale now at ShopRite for the small containers. If you're getting bare minimum, go for whatever gets you closest to 30.)
- Quart freezer bags: BJ's has them at 216-count for $17.29.
- Estimated cost of the lab: $6.98 (sugar) + $8.98 (whole milk) + $13.16 (half and half) + $23.96 (heavy cream) + $1.29 (fake vanilla) + $15.96 (salt) + $19.96 (more salt) + $7.98 (party cups) + $4.58 plastic spoons + $18.99 (gallon freezer bags) + $17.29 (quart freezer bags) = $139.13.

Note: My receipts this year add up to $103.68 but that doesn't count bags because I already had them.

Things to remind the students:
- Stuff you're going to eat goes into the quart bag.
- Ice goes into the gallon bag.
- The quart bag goes into the gallon bag. (Had a colleague whose students were shaking a bag of ice for 20 minutes and wondering why it didn't work. They had not put the inner bag inside the gallon bag.)

Other helpful tips and tricks:
- Cover two lab benches with paper towels. (If you don't have lab benches, pull 4-6 normal desks together facing each other. You need a large-ish flat area.)
- Ask for about 6-10 volunteers.

- Do the pouring yourself.

Happy mistakes:
- Made vanilla chai tea this afternoon. Accidentally put in the heavy cream. It was yummy, but not what I'd meant to use. I typically don't buy heavy cream because it's super expensive.

Takeaways:
- You can make ice cream with simple household ingredients.
- It makes a mess. Embrace the fact. Enjoy the chaos.
- It's expensive.

The kids always enjoy it. (Or they enjoy the day of me not yelling at them for their phones.)

Chapter 37:
Episode 157 – General Opinion: Beyond the Classroom Attending Extracurricular Activities

Introduction:

Dear Reader,

Gonna be honest. It's been a long while since I got myself to go to any school activities. Used to go to quite a bit.

Pre-pandemic, my friend and I would try to get to at least one game of most of the "normal" school sports that had home games and didn't require payment.

We made it to football, lacrosse, baseball, softball, soccer, tennis, and volleyball games.

The pandemic stopped that pretty much cold turkey.

Same for school plays and concerts. (Concerts are on my mind because apparently there's a big one coming up.)

Those things are largely back to normal now, but I started writing for Vella and kept myself on a crazy schedule.

But one of my students asked if I ever attend games. I told her I do sometimes.

So, I made the effort to show up.

Some current and former students saw me there. Watched both varsity and JV girls lacrosse games today.

(The varsity team won. The JV lost. It's fine. Was nice to see both teams.)

Though it can be difficult to see individual players, I have several students and former students who play.

One girl who can be hard to read emotionally plays goalie for the JV team. She had some nice saves. Will have to let her know I saw them. A friend who happens to be the JV coach said he had to give her a pep talk after the game. Losing can be difficult, especially if you have a key role on the team like goalie.

One of my other students is the star of the varsity team (at least one of the stars). Lost count of how many times she scored in the game. (Asked the coach I know, he said six.)

~Ann

Things I realized by watching the games this afternoon/evening:
- Lacrosse is an odd sport. Lots of starts, stops, and sprints.
- Stopping the clock every single time someone scores adds up to a lot of time. I think the first game legitimately went to an hour and a half.
- I had promised to see a JV game and those take place afterwards, but thankfully, they run a continuous clock.

- JV teams don't get the fancy scoreboard. That's terribly annoying.
- Lacrosse is a relatively high scoring game. I guess I'm just used to soccer where 1-2 is a typical score and 8 to 3 is a blowout.
- The first game was something like 20 to 12. Was close for most of the game. But then the home team had a comfortable-ish lead. I say -ish because it takes about 8 seconds for most of those goals.
- The JV game was messier. Resembled field hockey more, but it was still fun to watch.
- It's kind of a violent sport. Guess that goes with the territory of games with sticks. Guess there's good reason for the mouth guards. I don't think girls are required to wear a helmet unless they are goalie.
- I still don't know all the rules to that game. To be fair, this is like my 3rd lacrosse game ever. My school was too small to have a team.
- Not sure how more of the girls don't wreck their knees in that game. Or get dizzy.
- I regret not bringing my special butt cushion. It's been chilling in my car for 3 years. Thought I could stick out one game, but I have that thing for a reason and I'm too old to care what anybody thinks of me hauling that about. If I go to more games, I'm bringing the cushion.

Probably covered some of this ground before, but always good to ponder anew ...

Reasons to go see school sports, attend concerts, and whatnot:
- The students work hard at the extracurricular stuff.
- They enjoy seeing teachers there to watch their performances.

- Sports and plays are fun.
- If students think about teachers, I'm pretty sure they get a skewed view. They need to see teachers do normal people stuff, that includes showing your face in public at stuff they care about.
- People, in general, including high schoolers, enjoy attention. Part of the fun of creating and doing well is the good feeling and praise that goes along with it.
- Fresh air. (Okay, so it also comes with a side of allergens. Take a Claritin/Zyrtec/Allegra/knockoff allergy med and take one for the team.)
- It's good to see students in other context. Environment makes a huge difference. Some kids have a knack for annoying the crap out of you in their student guise, but as an athlete, they shine.
- Not saying it's going to magically fix all your woes, but it can give you a greater appreciation for other skills they have.
- Watching sports and concerts can be enjoyable. Go out to eat. Make a night of it.
- If your colleague's the coach, you can also support them.

Challenge for future me:
- Go see a wrestling match. Those are harder to get to because they're at weird times. Basketball too.
- Return to concerts. I used to chaperone them so I could watch and get paid. Might do it again, but it has conflicted mightily with my writing schedule.

Takeaways:
- Where possible, see the kids shine in other contexts.
- Everybody likes to have fans. That's part of the enjoyment of an accomplishment (being noticed).

- Kids need to see you out of the classroom as much as you need to see them out of the classroom.

Chapter 38:
Episode 158 – General Opinion:
Loving the Hard-to-Love Kid

Introduction:

Dear Reader,

Some topics are lighter. Some are heavier. This falls in the latter category.

Some kids are easier to love than others.

I've got a whole lot more to say about the changes in attitudes teachers are facing from students and parents.

But here, I'd like to discuss just one type of kid, one who's kind of hard to love.

Like vs. love:

First, a brief distinction between like and love.

Kids who follow directions and don't argue over every little point are, of course, more likable.

Love is a trickier beast.

Love is often harder but stronger.

The situation:
Midway through the year I got a new student. He should have been in a pullout room with a special program, but he adamantly opposed anything to do with special education.

I get it.

There can be a stigma attached to that. But I find the kids are in 3 camps:
- Don't want to be labeled special ed.
- Use it like a get-out-of-jail-free card.
- Very small percent – use it appropriately and get the help they need.

This student didn't do much of the work and generally got along with his classmates.

I was told from the beginning that I shouldn't really grade things for him. That was never put in writing. but it was heavily implied. Also, he never would have passed anything if he was graded normally.

He got very frustrated with the work. (Understandable, it was given at a level several above where he should have been placed.) But again, things were fine in my class because I didn't bother him about much.

Random mini-tales from my class:
- One time, he'd taken some kid's seat when the student got up to get something. The seat stealer just wouldn't move. He had a quiz to make up for me, so I called him over to take that. He willingly came over and started, got about 3

questions in, crumpled up the test, and tossed it in the garbage. He then put his head down on the desk.

- Another day, he was speaking German to the kids. He kept repeating one phrase. (I didn't know what it meant and the kids didn't seem too upset, so I let it go.)

Shortly thereafter, I got one of those cryptic admin notes that said the kid was suspended.

A few days later, got word he was suspended indefinitely.

Random Notes that only sort of made sense later:
- I noticed one day that my classroom was locked. They used to leave the magnets down. Now I have to use my key to get in.
- Someone melted a candle all over one of my ring stands. They also left the gas line to the fume hood open. (No way to know it was this kid.)
- The halls are gated after school promptly at 3:30.

General notes gathered about the kid after the fact:
- Showed up on school property while suspended. I think there was an incident in a History class that kind of set that ball in motion. I think this happened twice on the same day. (We had security camera photos.)
- Was speaking German, saying things like "Heil Hitler." (I think some seniors reported him saying this.)
- Cursed out the principal. (Big time.)
- Said drills are sort of a joke. (Okay, can't fault him too much there. They are sort of a joke.)
- Had teachers afraid of him. One teacher said she's glad she's in a supported classroom because there was another adult presence. (This is true. I never said that, but it makes sense. I 100% agree with the sentiment that I wouldn't

want to be in a class alone with this kid. Mostly, you just need a witness.)

- Was seen on a bike on school grounds.
- Talked about killing himself.
- Cops are on the lookout for him.
- That history incident. He'd been cursing out a kid and commenting on the other student's weight. The kid finally had enough and told him to shut the **** up.
- Both were taken to the office, but the teacher explained though the other kid isn't an angel by any stretch, here he was the victim of the initial harassment.
- Said the school is stupid. (Okay, I think half the teachers would agree at one point or another.) In this context, he was referring to one of those deadly boring assemblies. I think this one was about transgender students.
- Left an inappropriate private message on a teacher's Google classroom.

My thoughts/reflections:
- Clearly, this kid has some mental and social struggles.
- Indefinite suspension is just a way to get out of filing paperwork for an expulsion. I believe that reflects poorly on the school and can mess with funding. (Not just one, but a combination. It takes a LOT for them to expel someone.)
- It's a tough situation all around. On the one hand, you want to do the best you can for this kid. On the other hand, you need to protect your staff and other students from uncomfortable, untenable, and downright dangerous situations.
- There is no easy answer. Pray. Watch. Wait.
- I'm usually annoyed when schools get sued for something going wrong. The simple truth is that it's easy to say in hindsight, this or that should have been done, but

sometimes, there's no easy answer to how to help a troubled kid.

- One of my colleagues said that this kid's got a lot of the markings of a school shooter. A statement like that can (and probably should) spark healthy debate. But it's true. I remember when my colleague and I had that conversation, there had been a recent school shooting with a kid who came back after like 6 years. It might have been that Christian school one (The Covenant School in Nashville.)
- Not sure what the student is up to these days. Hope he finds the help he needs.
- So, back to my title point about love. Some people need more love and understanding than others, but these do not negate the need for consequences when behavior gets out of hand.

Takeaways:
- Some people are harder to love.
- Trouble has many sources.

Public schools strive to meet the needs of all students, but there are times when that leads to mutually exclusive paths, like removing one student from the school to safeguard others.

Chapter 39:
Episode 159 – End of Year Letters 2023

Introduction:

I have a tradition of writing a personal letter to each of my students.

During the pandemic, they were emails. I considered doing that this year because they are a hair easier. However, the hand-written part is part of the novelty. I'm not sure how many hand-written letters these kids will get in their lives now that stamps are crazy expensive and cursive writing isn't really taught.

I'm not sure I've ever clocked the hours it takes, but I can only do them in batches of 4-10-ish. Other than that, I risk hurting my hand.

Progress to date:
- Three of four classes done.
- 54 letters done.
- 16 more letters to go.

What do I say?

It varies, though there is definitely crossover. These are the general sentiments cropping up this year. Some statements are mutually exclusive.

- Thank you for participating. It is a tremendous help to me and you.
- Thanks for the answers you offered in class. Don't hesitate to keep on venturing answers. You have a lot of great things to add.
- Consider speaking up in class. You have much to add to the conversation.
- Learning is an active thing. The more you interact with material, the easier it will be.
- Hopefully, by the time you get this, we'll know you've made it through the class.
- You've done very well in a challenging class.
- Keep on working hard.
- Have you thought much about the future? (There's no right or wrong answer to that question. They're just different approaches.)
- Plan for the future but don't stress if things change.
- Enjoy the moment. High school will go quickly.
- Every stage of life has ups and downs.
- Surround yourself with good people, they will help you through harder times.
- Expect the best from yourself.
- Don't always take the easy road.
- I look forward to seeing what you become in the future. (I feel odd saying that because it sounds like I mean life begins later, which isn't true.)
- *I usually pick 2 songs for them off the playlist. The list created for this year isn't my favorite. I think I prefer last

year's list, but this one also isn't done. I've added at least 5 songs since starting to write the letters.

Where do I go?

I've taken to going to Starbucks or Panera. It's a lot easier to push stuff off if I have my computer handy.

Not taking my computer forces me to do what I set out to do, which is usually a batch of letters.

They play music but I have AirPods. I also have a playlist to listen to that was made for the current batch of students.

It's always nice to have an excuse to go for a long walk. The Starbucks by my apartment is about a mile away, so I get fresh air and time to work in peace. All around win.

Sometimes, I need to add a song to the list.

I thought I already wrote that one up, but I'll probably have to cover it in one of the review collections.

What kinds of songs are on the list?

The list features League of Legends, Lindsey Stirling, The Sidh, Taylor Davis, Tommee Profitt, Liv Ash, SVRCINA, Cameron James, Sam Tinnesz, Aiden Appleton, Andreas Kubler, me, Liz Brand, Zayde Wolfe, and many others.

Why me?

I included a few of my songs and suggested them to a few of the more creative students. I used it as an example to do whatever they want in life.

I'd had a small goal of getting something available on Spotify. A few years ago, I made it happen. (It's not as glamourous as you think, but it's still cool.)

Do I think everybody should do this?

No. If you want to, go for it, but if the thought fills you with dread, find some other way to reach out that works for you.

My colleague uses a poem she found online and prepares little care packages for her students during the final.

I'm more inclined to give them the letter during one of the review days and then hand out lollipops during the final itself.

Point is, do what works for you.

Takeaways:
- Doing something special for your students doesn't have to be expensive.
- It's more about thought and care.
- Find something that works with your personality.
- This can also apply in other areas of life. While I was in the letter-writing mode, I also wrote my colleague to encourage her.

Chapter 40:
Episode 160 – General Opinion:
Terrible Sick Days Policies

Introduction:
Dear Reader,

I've definitely run afoul of the restrictions on when and where and how we take days off.

I understand there's some validity to having restrictions in terms of needs unique to staffing a school.

There's still a shortage of teachers and substitutes overall. I think the moral of my story here is going to be teachers shouldn't be penalized for having families and lives outside of their districts.

This might turn into a mini-series here about the contentious relationship that exists between districts and their employees. (**Spoiler:** Laws like this don't improve that relationship.)

Pulled the inspiration for this Chapter from a Facebook post. Will paraphrase.

Original poster was looking for someone familiar with the law in New Jersey that says teachers can't use sick days to take care of their children.

~Ann

Pertinent points:

- Woman's kid got sick, had to be put in the hospital, and had to have surgery.
- While in the hospital, she got messages from her school that she needed a doctor's note or risk being written up for "theft of days" and brought up on tenure charges.
- The anxiety of sick kiddo was not helped at all by worry about getting into trouble for taking off. (The whole situation made the lady lose sleep and tremble with anger at having needlessly been stuck in the situation by an unfeeling law.)
- Union's answer (echoed by the masses on Facebook) – go get a doctor's note for yourself.
- Poster's problem – I shouldn't have to lie. Wasn't on a beach. Was at the hospital with my kid. (Had already used the 3 family sick days earlier on her other child getting the flu.)
- There's the possibility of Family Medical Leave Act but that would involve a pay cut for those days off when she had perfectly good sick days available.

My response:

I 100% agreed with the majority of the advice. The stress the situation put her under officially moved her into the can't-work-today status. No lies needed.

I do agree that needing a doctor's note to prove mental stress is on the ridiculous side. But needs must and all.

It would be far worse for this lady to have to take a $1000 pay cut to stay with her kid.

Will some people abuse a nicer policy?

Maybe. (Oh, who am I kidding? Of course.)

That said, teachers are wired to get stuff done. Nobody likes feeling like they are unprepared, so we as a species tend to go well out of our way to be as prepared as possible so our classes function at the highest possible capacity.

Even if someone's inclined to abuse a policy like this, I can almost guarantee you they will leave adequate work and deal with the fallout from crazy classes later if they're gone too long.

Will it change?

Being me, I Googled it and found a March 24, 2023 article talking about a similar sick day situation. Will likely use it for a responses Chapter on the topic, but the gist of that one is that a lady couldn't use her sick days to visit her dying mother. (The amendment is up before a committee, which is the first step before going to the state senate. I believe the article said it cleared the first hurdle.)

Conclusion:

Policies are cold-hearted. There should be more wiggle room about extenuating circumstances. People get sick. Their kids get sick. Sick days should certainly extend more to family. There are three days of family sick leave built into many systems, but if you have more than one kid or if you have sick folks, it's not exactly something you can halt because three days is your max.

Takeaways:

- Sick kiddos can't exactly take care of themselves all the time, especially if the sickness is taking them to a hospital.
- Policies are in place to protect the institution, which is all well and good to a point, but compassion and common sense needs to also prevail.

Chapter 41:
Episode 161 – Teacher Advice for Managing Parents (with Commentary)

Introduction:
Dear Reader,
I don't always agree with every article WeAreTeachers puts out, but this one seems interesting.

Most of the advice is common sense, and not everything is available or enjoyable to all people. That said, it's nice to have the list in one place.

Also, some advice is only applicable at certain ages.

~Ann

The Advice: (Things teachers have done.)
Build a foundation right away with positive communication:
- Send parents pictures of their kid having fun (would only recommend up through elementary school).
- I send an intro email to parents before the school year and then positive updates when I can.

- Share good news.
- Kids enjoy being talked about in a good light.

My response to build-a-foundation:
- Agree, but find something that works for you.
- I do a weekly newsletter for both students and parents. The student one is posted to their class website. The parent one is emailed. These take me about 1-2 hours to arrange but that's because I need to figure out the lesson plan first. The letter-writing part is probably less.
- The first letter talks about the importance of communication.
- One of my first assignments is a communications project. Part of that includes a parent/guardian emailing me the answer to a simple question. I then give them a piece of information to convey to their kid. Kid then does a project for me. It's more about opening those lines of communication than anything else.

Proof parents appreciate it:
- Usually a very nice parent email at the end of the year.
- Less stressful communication throughout the year. (This isn't a guarantee. People can and will still pull the crazy parent card occasionally.)

Create transparency via regular updates:
- Send a weekly email with test/quiz reminders and a trivia question. (Person said this takes them 10 minutes.)
- Made a class Instagram account. (Got a LOT of permissions to make this happen.)

My response to the regular updates via a social media account:
- My school would likely not go for that.

- If you want to try it, definitely get permissions. Also, be super careful about what you post.

Set and stand by boundaries:
- Stick to the workday hours.
- Never email or call on weekends.
- See if your district has a policy about how quickly you need to respond. (It's normally 24-48 hours.) Don't respond to hostile things until you're an hour from that deadline.

My response to set and keep boundaries:
- Mostly disagree personally.
- I've always responded when I want to. Generally, that is night and weekends when I'm not trying to juggle something else.
- I agree with the point of not responding immediately if you're upset, but I wouldn't want to wait until a specified time.

Invest in Relationships:
- Go to concerts, games, and other stuff when you can. Person noted it's harder to be rude to someone who came to support your kid.
- Perspective: One teacher pointed out that anger over a grade is a fear of failure or not getting into a good college.
- Common theme: Be proactive.

My response to relationships via school spirit activities:
- Used to do a lot more.
- The pandemic changed a lot of that for me. I did make it to few lacrosse games this year, but that's about it.
- Also been skipping out on chaperoning the concerts because my Vella writing schedule got busy.

- Missed all the school plays this year. I was away for one of them.
- It's still a fantastic idea but go with what works for you. Some people can't make it because they have family obligations. Others are busy with other life stuff.

Takeaways:

- Getting to know people is important in any arena.
- Having open lines of communication is important for working with parents.

You can't control all the crazy. Some will still crawl out from somewhere and bite you, but manage what you can by being personable and real with people.

Chapter 42:
Episode 162 – 22-23 Songs for Students Playlist Explained Part 1

Introduction:

Dear Reader,

Whoops. Well, I was going to do a post about graduation. Yeah, I know we're late. My entire state runs late compared to much of the country. And homeschoolers. They do whatever the heck they want.

So, instead, you get my playlist thoughts.

This is the 2022 – 2023 playlist. I might try to do the next one early, but really, it makes sense to do the recap instead of the beginning. When I write my letters to the students, I tend to add more songs.

Sometimes, a song fits a student, just one. Other times, a song fits many students.

Might have to split the list a bit.

~Ann

22-23 Songs for Students Playlist (and commentary):

1. Dragonmancer – 2021 by League of Legends – This one has been on a few of my lists. It's a nice introductory song. Starts out slow, ominous even.
2. Mural Legends by Adriel Fair – Light and cheery but not too cheery.
3. Holy – String Ensemble by The Bedtime Orchestra – Soft, contemplative, would be good to work with this in the background.
4. The Wild Air by Joni-Fuller, Power-Haus – More stringed instruments; light, adventuresome.
5. Ocean Eyes by J.T. Peterson – This is montage music for learning something at least at the start.
6. Ice Storm by Lindsey Stirling – I've always said she has a very unique style. It tends to be more upbeat and off beat at the same time (compared to other violinists.)
7. Will the Circle Be Unbroken by AtinPiano – Soft piano piece. Nice to come to after a Lindsey Stirling song because it slows things down. This one is very relaxing.
8. Departure to the West (Princess Monoke) by Eliott Tordo Erhu – I didn't like the movie when I saw it ages ago, but the song is good. Soft, yet full of restrained life.
9. From Father to Son by The Sidh – This one picks up the pace. Because of the title, I only picked it for some of the boys, but honestly, it just fit the young men I picked anyway. Upbeat. Full of promise.
10. Underground by Lindsey Stirling – I don't usually have two songs by the same artist so close together. This one starts medium and picks up the pace about 45 seconds in.
11. Gerudo Valley From the Ocarina Of Time by Taylor Davis – This is my other favorite violin player. She tends to do more covers of stuff. Also very talented. This one is

beautiful. Quicker paced than many songs, but maybe not quite as frenetic as a Lindsey Stirling song.

12. For Eternity by IMAscore – Slows the pace down quite a bit. Back to thinking style music.

13. Eversong by Epic Score, Snorre Tidemand – Epic fantasy type theme. Background choral stuff. Would expect to be marching towards a dragon's lair to do battle or gearing up for a giant invasion.

14. Guitar Chronicle by Autodidactic studios, Waterflame, pftq – Light. Fun. Motivating.

15. High Seas by Pauli Hausmann – Does in fact give the feel of good maritime music. Sea adventure. It's also soft enough to stay in the background.

16. Teutates by Tartalo Music – Faster. Scottish. Kind of a cheery theme.

17. Ready to Go by Liv Ash – This is the first song on the list that has lyrics. Motivating. Not exactly humble. Kind of music to run out onto a field with. Good exercise music is how I think one of my students put it once.

18. Face the Fire by Shangrii-La – Also has lyrics. Seems to speaks about overcoming something tough.

19. A Storm Is Comin by Tommee Profitt, Liv Ash – Another prepare for something type song. Not a huge amount of lyrics. I do love Liv Ash's voice.

20. Hard To Breathe by UNSECRET, Samantha Tieger – Facing hardship. Ha, sometimes I think that's how my students view the class.

21. Where We Rise by Neoni – Don't remember much about this one. Slow start. Sounds like gearing up for battle. Proving oneself.

22. Show You by Cameron James – This one also doesn't lack in the self-confidence category.

23. Who Are You (Russ Macklin Remix) by SVRCINA, Russ Macklin – I've heard both versions, but I think I heard this one first. A friend introduced me to SVRCINA ages ago. She's awesome. Pretty sure one or more of her songs makes it to almost every one of my playlists.

Guess I should cut it off here since the list goes on for another 23 songs. They're usually not quite so long. Not sure why I added a lot more to the end of the list.

Will put the link in the note so you can check it out if you want.

Chapter 43:
Episode 163 – 22-23 Songs for Students Playlist Explained Part 2

Introduction:

Dear Reader,

Time to continue the list of songs compiled for this past year's students.

We just got to the songs that have lyrics. I typically put mostly instrumental in the beginning, then whatever comes for songs with lyrics, then finish with some instrumental stuff.

I think the last song has lyrics, but that's because it was a very recent addition to the list. I may have to shuffle some of the songs for best playing effect.

I've marked where the normal list ended before I added for one reason or another.

~Ann

22-23 Songs for Students Playlist continued:

24. It's Going Down Undefeated by Devin Hoffman, Richard Vegas, Jessica Easley – Smooth but upbeat. Motivating. I have recommended this song to many students over the years. It's on a few of the student lists.

25. With You Til The End by Tommee Profitt, Sam Tinnesz – Recommended this to quite a few students too. It's beautiful. Love this guy's voice too.

26. Believer by Tommee Profitt, Colton Dixon – Starts out whimsical. This is a cover.

27. Jumpin' In by Oh The Larceny – I've started out a different list with this. It's a good opener. Motivational and catchy. Basically about jumping into something full-force.

28. My Turn Now by Hidden Citizens, VE – I think the album is dystopian or something. Standing out.

29. Peace of God – Kevin Kraft Instrumental Remix by Julie C. Gilbert, Kevin M. Kraft – Back to instrumental stuff. Peaceful. Also has a contemplative feel to it.

30. Pure Eudiamonia by Really Slow Motion, Instrumental Core – Some songs just fit together. This is a very nice one to follow Peace of God. It takes that vibe and expands on it.

31. Pacific Coast Highway by Aiden Appleton, Marcus Warner – Road trip adventure. Like you're headed into the unknown.

32. Together We Are Free by Andreas Kubler – For some reason, this is a nice pairing with Pacific Coast Highway. I've ended at least one playlist with this song. It's a nice finisher. It's on a list about a pair of guardian angels in training. Somehow it was a very good theme song for them. Strength together. One of my favorite instrumental songs.

33. Lunar Revel 2022: Almost Home by League of Legends: Wild Rift – This flows nicely from Together We Are Free.

It's a little faster. Has lovely flow. I believe this used to be the end of the list. After this, I added songs that fit particular students. Some songs weren't even published when I first compiled the list.

34. Crowned Kings by Dream Cave – Probably should be up near the beginning of the list. (I may reorder.) Sounds like the main character is gearing up to face demons or something.

35. Healer's Love (Kalastan) – Features Liz Brand by Julie C. Gilbert, Liz Brand – Liz has a lovely voice. Acapella. Probably the only unaccompanied song on the list.

36. Speechless by Lydia the Bard, Frostudio Chambersonic – I don't think I could actually finish the song, but it fit the notion of standing up for yourself. I might remove this one.

37. Jade Princess by John Adamich – Also a current favorite. Like you're getting ready for a fantasy adventure.

38. Brawl Stars Main Menu Theme by Greatest Bits – Sounds like an 80's video game. That's by design. I've recommended this one to a few of my gamers.

39. Neon Night by Joseph William Morgan – Goes with the previous song. Literally from an album called 80's Action.

40. Rey's Theme by John Williams – Spotify has a lightsaber as the progress bar. That's awesome. You can call Rey out for being a Mary Sue but she's still a fun character and very cute plushie. (I collect random cheap Star Wars junk. Everybody has a vice.) Story might have been somewhat weak, but John Williams still came through with excellent music.

41. Planet and Comets by Celestial Aeon Project, Tuomas Nikkinen – A very short song, but has the promise of exploration. Might be near the start of next year's list too.

42. Born Ready by Zayde Wolf – One with lyrics. Probably should move this. Zayde's another favorite. His songs are

a bit more in-your-face than many of the others. Recommended to many students. They have a lot of inner strength they don't tap.

43. Ocean Champions by Derek Fiechter, Brandon Fiechter – Probably the first and only song I've ever heard about Mermen. (That's the album title.) Noble. Strong.

44. Born to Be a Leader by Amadeus Indetzki – You'll notice some of the overlap in songs from ones I made for my superhero book. This is another, go-get-'em sort of song.

45. Assemble Legends by Brand X Music – Actually makes more sense at the beginning. This album is definitely geared to accompanying superheroes. Love the energy in the song. Has a strong fighting-evil-and-standing-for-good vibe.

46. Thumbs by Sabrina Carpenter – I have Kate S. to thank for the discovery of this song. It has amazing lyrics. Kind of a heavy/ serious thought to leave the students with. Don't be someone who just twiddles your thumbs.

Takeaways:

- Music sets moods very well.
- Some songs stand out for certain students.
- Some songs just stand for an idea I hope the class conveys to them.

Chapter 44:
Episode 164 – General Opinion: How to Respond to the Wanna-be Influencers

Introduction:
Dear Reader,

This is probably going to be formatted more like one of the general response sort of articles.

Found it on WeAreTeachers.com. Decided to put it here because I'd meant to write an article about the topic anyway.

~Ann

Article Title: Help! My Students Say They Don't Need School Because They're Going to Be Influencers
By Kelly Treleaven
July 7, 2023

The Issue:
- Students (high school juniors) don't think they need

Algebra II because they're going to be TikTok stars.

- (Ha, the anonymous tag is Bubble-Burster.)

WeAreTeachers response:

- The responder's students wanted to be NBA stars. The responder made two contracts, talked with the kids about them, and show them how both were terrible if you read closely.
- Responder wanted to show them that the teacher's dream for the kids and their dream for themselves could fit together. Didn't want to be the cold reality check.
- Offered some math-specific types of problems and provided a handy dandy link to an article on how much influencers make.
- Have a motive to not squash their dreams but to show them how to frame their version of success. (What does it take to make a living as an influencer?)

There were other issues, but I'll stick with this one for now.

Relevant bunny trail: What does it take to make it as a social media star? (Or at least what do they make annually?)

Article from Franklin.edu. (Not sure when, it didn't say in an easy-to-find spot.)

Their stats were from 2021.

- Jobs in 2021 = 6700.
- Average compensation $41,142.
- Job posting demands: 3,550 (This is how many jobs were available.)
- Highest influencers earned about $65,832, lowest made about $26,333.
- Hourly, high pay was $32 and low was $13 with an average of $20.

- They also had a chart of the last 3 years and the salaries are all over the place.
- The chart for growth in the industry projected about 95 jobs being added by 2031. (That doesn't sound like a lot.)

(7/12/23) My response to the article about jobs as an influencer.

- First, I think there's a misconception about earnings.
- The kids who want a career as an influencer are really only picturing the dozen or so superstar success cases where hypothetical YouTubers retire from their toy review job at age 17 earning $50K a month.
- As the responder from WeAreTeachers noted, kids probably didn't factor in the cost of living.
- One of my former students was actually an influencer as a high schooler. He designed and sold T-shirts. I think it was good pocket money but nothing he could live off of yet.

What should a teacher do?

- There is a temptation to laugh in their delusional little faces, but teachers do wield a lot of psychological power. Probably best to be gentle. (For many, it's about as realistic as getting an AI generated book and making it to the New York Times Bestseller list or even pouring heart and soul into one book and becoming an instant millionaire. Possible? Sure. Realistic? Not really.)
- Gentle reality check 1: The odds aren't in their favor, generally speaking. Will there be super success stories? Of course. If they are good at it, they have earning potential, but money isn't everything.
- Gentle reality check 2: The algorithm can change in a heartbeat. You're going to want to/need to diversify to make it. Markets get flooded. Things change. Companies

go under and/or get bought out. (Never a great idea to have all your eggs in one basket.)

- Gentle reality check 3: Life skills are rarely wasted. For many subjects, the *when will I ever use this question* answer is probably never, but school is about so much more than the academics. It's about social sense, responsibility, self-discipline, doing hard things, and time management. School is good practice for problem solving. People skills are needed in every profession, especially being an influencer.
- Gentle reality check 4: When you turn something into a job, you usually have to work. The notion of always having to perform/produce can be draining.
- Gentle reality check 5: You may love your job, but there will always be things you won't like about your job. With social media, you'll get trolls. People will say mean and unreasonable things to you and about you. You're putting yourself out there, so expect comments.
- Gentle reality check 6: (Probably don't say this to their faces unless you want parent emails.) Beauty fades. Even if you make stellar money right now, your 17-year-old self will grow up. When you're 27, the 17-year-olds will think you're over-the-hill. You'll have to grow with your audience.

Takeaways:
- Dreams and goals are awesome, but don't let any one dream prevent you from diversifying your skillset.
- Adaptation and growth don't go away.
- Being an influencer is hard work.

Chapter 45:
Episode 165 – General Response:
Random Expectations Placed
on Teachers

Introduction:

Dear Reader,

Teachers get asked to do a lot of things that aren't exactly covered by the handbook.

As a profession, we tend to be good with doing with less or inventing a way on a shoestring budget.

But what do you do when the principal asks something of you. (Depends on the ask.)

~Ann

Quick definition: Voluntold – being essentially told you're going to volunteer for a position.

Story 1: How to conjure tennis balls. School got new floors. Teachers told by principal they should protect said new floors.

The suggestion was with tennis balls.

The response to Story 1 from WeAreTeachers:
- Invite the principal to realize that teachers probably don't have access to the sheer number of tennis balls needed to protect the floors from the desks.
- Other advice: wait a week or two.
- Estimated cost would be $100-$200. Unrealistic to ask teachers to cover that cost themselves.

(7/12/23) My response to Story 1:
- Sounds like a buildings and grounds thing.
- If I was doing this on a nothing budget, I'd probably opt for buying actual felt and packing tape. Not sure how well it would work. Might explore if cardboard would work. Who cares if it's ugly. It's not your home. Play cheap games, get cheap solutions.
- Would also ask around at a fabric store, sometimes they have cheap useless pieces of scrap that might work.
- But before testing the boundaries of creativity, I'd politely try to point out this ain't my problem. If they could shell out for a new floor, they can pony up for floor protection.

Story 2: Teacher voluntold to lead the high school's Model U.N.
The response to Story 2 from WeAreTeachers:
- Responder tells the teacher they too were once told they were going to head something they had no experience with. (That time it was robotics.)
- Reframe: you and the students can learn about it together
- Ask the principal for support.
- Work exactly 1 day on learning the Model U.N. via videos online.

(7/12/23) My response to Story 2:

- I probably shouldn't put into the universe that I've mostly escaped that fate when it comes to extracurriculars.
- I was scheduled to teach an elementary class while in a private Christian school. That was a disturbing change of pace.
- There are always things that need doing and *for the kids* only goes so far. Part of the unwritten (and probably not healthy) culture of schools is you do whatever you can to convince the higher ups to keep you until you pass that tenure threshold.
- First, this shouldn't happen. I know it's difficult to get people to volunteer for stuff, but people who are coerced or pressured into things don't typically develop a deep abiding passion for the thing they're semi-forced to do.
- If you can, just say no. (A lot of new teachers have this fear of being let go for no good reason and want to make themselves look good. Hard to turn stuff down when you think it might be the difference between having and not having a job. That scene from the Muppet's Christmas Carol comes to mind. The one where the rats are complaining about lack of coal. Scrooge threatens to fire them. They say something like "Heat wave! This is my island in the sun!" The point being, suddenly bad conditions are good when faced with an alternative of unemployment. If you're untenured, they don't even need a good excuse to get rid of you.)
- Awhile back, the science supervisor was hunting for an advisor for one of those science testing clubs. Was a game of dodge-the-supervisor there for a while.
- There was a meme recently with a little girl. In the left picture she looks neat and ordered. In the right picture, the same kid is bawling. It says something like when your

principal calls you to tell you they're switching levels. On the phone (left pic) and off the phone (right pic). I think it was more about switching elementary school grades, but the same could be true for being told you're volunteering to head a random club.

- In some schools there is a stipend for many clubs, but the hours vs. the compensation don't usually work out in the teacher's favor.
- Saying no is super hard, but sometimes, it's necessary.

Takeaways:
- Sometimes no is the best response (and the hardest)
- There are probably cheap solutions to protecting the floors, but I am not convinced that problem should be a responsibility placed upon teachers.

Chapter 46:
Episode 166 – Brain Break: My Response to Random Debate Questions from WeAreTeachers Part 1

Introduction:
Dear Reader,

Sometimes, you just need a change of pace.

Found these debate topics under the classroom ideas (random link) at the bottom of the WeAreTeachers site.

Original list by Jill Staake from July 7, 2022.

~Ann

Random debate topics and my personal opinion:
- Topic: Hot dogs are sandwiches.
- My response: Well, I Googled the definition of a sandwich. Google says a sandwich is food with two pieces of bread with meat, cheese, or other filling between them. So, maybe. You'd have to accept a bun as bread and probably

break the backside so that the hotdog is trapped between the two halves.

- Topic: Tacos are sandwiches.
- My response: False. Given the definition, you'd have to qualify the taco shell (soft or hard) as bread, which is a bit of a stretch. If you broke open the back end ... maybe.
- Topic: French fries must have ketchup.
- My response: That's how I like them. A little salt and some ketchup, but it's not absolutely necessary to have. People's tastes differ. I've also put some hot sauce on fries. That was yummy.
- Topic: Pepperoni is the best topping for pizzas.
- My response: Eh, it's okay. Not my favorite. I'm a pineapple and ham kind of person, though I also love a good margarita or peppers and onions or black olives or meat lover's pizza. About all I won't go for is anchovies.
- Topic: Peanut butter trumps Nutella.
- My response: For me, yes. Nutella has its uses, but peanut butter is much more versatile.
- Topic: Hot chocolate bests chocolate milkshakes.
- My response: I'm a vanilla shake fan personally, but I don't get the comparison. They're used in completely different context. If it's 90°F outside, I'm not choosing hot chocolate. Likewise, if it's freezing out, I'm probably not rushing out to get a chocolate milkshake.
- Topic: Fruit can be dessert.
- My response: Absolutely. Especially if there's whipped cream involved.
- Topic: Coke is better than Pepsi.
- My response: I don't usually drink either of the normal versions. They're both really sweet. I know that's a tad hypocritical because my favorite sodas are Dr. Pepper and a few select brands of root beer. If I had to choose, I'd

probably go Pepsi. It's crisper. But both will take your teeth out without a second glance.

- Topic: Round pizza trumps rectangle pizza.
- My response: Mostly true, but that's because the superior brands tend to make round pizzas. Are we talking frozen pizzas? So, rectangle pizza that pops to mind for frozen is Ellio's. If I'm comparing that to Red Baron, I'm going to laugh you out of the room.
- Topic: Ice cream trumps cake.
- My response: Mostly true. Never was much of a cake fan. I'd much rather have ice cream or cookies.
- Topic: McDonald's is the best fast-food.
- My response: Depends what you're in the mood for. Straight fry competition, maybe. Overall, I'm leaning Chick Fil A.
- Topic: Chocolate is better than vanilla flavored ice cream.
- My response: I prefer vanilla. It's a tad milder and more versatile. So, how are we defining better.
- Topic: Humans should eat to live, not live to eat.
- My response: Huh? Eating is necessary for life, but nothing says it has to be drudgery. There's an art to better meals. Like anything, it can be a form of expression.
- Topic: Chocolate chip cookies are the best.
- My response: I like snickerdoodles better. But they gotta be a specific kind. From stores, eh, I also like oatmeal and those Mint Milano cookies.
- Topic: Hot chocolate vs eggnog, HC wins.
- My response: Agreed. But that's mostly because I really do not like eggnog more than I think there's much special about hot chocolate.
- Topic: You shouldn't put ketchup on a hot dog.
- My response: I'm gonna put it on anyway. I happen to like it.

- Topic: Don't put pineapple on pizza.
- My response: Cool. I'll take your extra pineapple. It's really yummy. Has a nice blend of sweet to counterbalance the rest of the pizza.
- Topic: Mac and cheese can't be eaten with a fork.
- My response: I like stabbing the noodles. It's cooler than looking like an idiot chasing the noodles around the plate.
- Topic: Cereal goes in, then milk goes in.
- My response: I do it the other way to make less of a mess and because I'm particular about the ratio of milk to cereal. My way, milk first, means I get crispier cereal.

Takeaways:

- Ice cream rules.
- Milk in first won't kill you.
- Pineapple is perfectly functional as a pizza topping.

Chapter 47:
Episode 167 – Brain Break: My Response to Random Debate Questions from WeAreTeachers Part 2

Introduction:
Dear Reader,

Welcome back. We're still on a bit of a summer brain break.
~Ann

General debate topics: (I think debate is the wrong term. It should be discussion because they're 100% random opinions with 0 stakes.)

- Topic: Families should have a pet.
- My response: That's a stupid generalization. Pets aren't random things you can indulge in and then forget about. They are living beings that require a heck of a lot of upkeep. Pets are nice, but many families either aren't in the right financial situation or do not have the time to devote to a pet.
- Topic: Dogs are better pets than cats.

- My response: Depends what you like. Cats can be lower maintenance, but that's not always true.
- Topic: Summer is better than winter.
- My response: Well, I'm 100% biased here. Summers mean a different kind of work for me, one that does not involve school. So, yes, summers are better than winter. If we're talking about the weather, then I do prefer winter because it's a heck of a lot easier to layer up than down.
- Topic: Candy is a good classroom reward.
- My response: It can be. You need to be careful about allergies. Dum Dums are made in an allergy-free (meaning no tree nuts and such) facility. Would avoid chocolate for many reasons. Also, certain classrooms like labs should not have food stuffs for the kids unless they're leaving. They should not get used to eating in lab classes.
- Topic: Clowns are scary not funny.
- My response: Clowns are creepy. Creepy doesn't necessarily translate to scary, but it can.
- Topic: Modern music trumps classical music.
- My response: I don't think I strictly like either. I prefer video game style instrumental music, so I guess that leans more of a modern-ish take on classical stuff.
- Topic: Xbox is better than PlayStation.
- My response: My Xbox is downright ancient. I don't know enough about either of the latest iterations of the systems. I tapped out right around the time they wanted you to switch to a monthly subscription. I like reviewing stuff, but I don't have the time to devote to video games anymore.
- Topic: (American) Football is better than soccer.
- My response: In what context? Watching? Playing? Watching, yes, I'd agree American football is more fun to watch. Soccer (football to the rest of the world) is more fun to play a pickup game.

- Topic: Everyone should make their bed.
- My response: It's a good habit. It's nice to have routines to prepare mentally for the day. Making the bed is a good one.
- Topic: It would be better to fly than turn invisible.
- My response: I've probably spent more time thinking about superpowers than most people due to another one of my Vellas. I'd agree, but you also have to talk about the context. If you're trying to sneak into a place, Invisibility would serve you better. In terms of sheer fun, I think flying would be more fun, but there's a greater chance of being crapped on by birds. Invisibility sound stressful because you have to be more aware of your surroundings, lest you get run over by pedestrians who can't see you.
- Topic: People should be allowed to wander anywhere barefoot.
- My response: False.
- First, people aren't allowed to go just any place for good reason. Construction zones aren't safe for most types of footwear, let alone none.
- Second, stores already bear some responsibility for the welfare of their customers. That gives them the right to ask for—and enforce—rules like thou shalt wear shoes in our establishment. You might be perfectly safe, but you could also accidentally get your foot run over with a cart. It's a bigger deal if you're barefoot.
- Third, many restaurants that are way out of my comfortable price range have dress codes. Their house, their rules. If you don't want to abide by those rules, you are welcome to take your money elsewhere.
- Topic: Fiction is better than nonfiction.
- My response: If you'd asked me this a year ago, I would have agreed wholeheartedly, but in reading a bunch of

Vellas, I find the nonfiction way more interesting. Maybe I'm just old.

- Topic: Everyone should learn to play a musical instrument.
- My response: Everyone should at least attempt to see if they like playing a musical instrument. Hard facts are not everybody's going to be good at it. They won't know until they try, so there should be some effort put into trying. Music has much to teach us about discipline and control and nuance. It's not the only pursuit that can reinforce those lessons though.
- Topic: Werewolves are more dangerous than vampires.
- My response: I'm going to go with whichever one I'm facing at the moment is probably the most dangerous. But if you look at the stereotypical powersets given to werewolves and vampires, vamps might come out on top. To the average human, both would be deadly. Weird comparison.
- Topic: People shouldn't have to go to school or work on their birthdays.
- My response: A birthday is just a day. You can celebrate at a different time if needed. It's nice if you can take the day off. (I have a summer birthday, so I've typically had the birthday off.) Nice if it works out, but if it doesn't, make up for it with a celebration on a different day.
- Topic: It's better to be the superhero than the sidekick.
- My response: Depends how much you like responsibility. The sidekick is more likely to be kidnapped. The superhero draws most of the attention both good and bad. Attention can be overwhelming very quickly.
- Topic: Books are better than movies.
- My response: Not really a fair comparison because they are very different mediums. Generally, yes, but that's because books tend to be longer. Also, it depends on the book or

series. For Star Wars, you get different stories in book form than most of the movies. In Lord of the Rings, I saw the movies first, so I prefer those. In Harry Potter, I'd probably go movies because I can get the story scope in overall less time than I'd have to devote to the book series.

And I like audiobooks better than ebooks because of the time-saving aspects.

- Topic: Snow skiing is better than water skiing.
- My response: Very different experiences. Better in which context? Sheer exhilaration, water skiing probably wins.
- Topic: Never wear socks with sandals.
- My response: I do because I'm usually in socks. If I'm in sandals, I'm probably running up to get the mail or bring down the recycling bin. Not there for the fashion sense. There because I don't want to ruin my socks on my errand.

Takeaways:

- Socks with sandals might not be high fashion, but since I don't give a fig, I'm gonna do it anyway.
- I'd rather be a superhero.
- Fiction and nonfic have their uses. Both can be entertaining.

Chapter 48:
Episode 168 – Brain Break: My Response to Random Debate Questions from WeAreTeachers Part 3

Introduction:
Dear Reader,

This was all one long list of questions, but thankfully, it was already broken down by sections.

It was kind of fun answering these. I may have to subject others to the experience.

~Ann

General Discussion Topics for Older students:
- Topic: Pluto should be considered a planet.
- My response: Yes. Next.
- Topic: Santa Claus's elves should be paid minimum wage.
- My response: If you're making toys for all the world's kids, you should be making way more than minimum wage.
- Topic: There's intelligent life on other planets.

- My response: Honey, sometimes, I doubt there's intelligent life on this planet. Sentient life, maybe.
- Topic: The egg came before the chicken.
- My response: Doesn't matter. My guess is chicken came first with the ability to form the egg. Adam and Eve were created in adult status (or my understanding of Genesis is screwed up). It makes sense other creatures would be created as adult status.
- Topic: Harry Potter is better than The Lord of the Rings.
- My response: You keep saying better, but better in what way? A better story? Maybe. A better movie series. Probably not. I liked both. Book-wise, I liked HP better but that's because it's simpler to understand. Tolkien went deep with the language and side stuff. It made for a rich world, but it also takes a lot more mental capacity to dig through. If I'm in it for the entertain-me-because-I-don't-want-to-think, I'm going Harry Potter.
- Topic: The world would be better if women were always in charge.
- My response: Another stupid generalization. It depends fully on what woman, as it depends on what man, is in charge. Some women, sure, stuff would get done and done well. Other women, you'd be lucky to get anything done.
- Topic: It's better to be TikTok famous than Instagram famous.
- My response: I don't intend to try for either. In terms of money, probably. They have different audiences. I think TikTok's skews a hair younger.
- Topic: Facebook should add a "Don't Like" button.
- My response: They do. It's just a sad face or an angry face. It asks you to qualify what you don't like. I'm going to go with the notion that they don't need more buttons. Though I would like a ginormous question mark if we're taking

requests. More often than not, I don't need a *don't like*, I need a *what-the-heck-does-this-mean* button.

- Topic: Aliens are living among us here on Earth.
- My response: Aliens as in little green men? Probably not.
- Topic: Using curse words is no big deal.
- My response: Curse words are like really strong spice. If you use them too often, they're just going to make a big stink everywhere. Depends on the context and setting. In a school, they should not be used. Overusing them makes it sound like you're too lazy to figure out how to express yourself.
- Topic: Bottled water is better than tap water.
- My response: That depends on who's bottling the water, where it comes from, and what kind of treatment the tap water got. I'm pretty sure if we got some chemical kits, we wouldn't like what's in either.
- Topic: Going out is more fun than staying in at home.
- My response: False. (Card carrying introvert here.) Going out can be fun, but it also takes effort.
- Topic: Daydreaming trumps night dreaming.
- My response: Pretty sure those are very different things. Well, I get chased less during daydreams.
- Topic: All's fair in love and war.
- My response: Ha. Things are rarely fair in either love or war. There are some rules both spoken and unspoken, but people have played dirty in both.
- Topic: Robin Hood is a thief and should not be considered a hero.
- My response: This is true for any hero. If you're the rich person being stolen from so Robin Hood can re-distribute the wealth, yeah, dude's a thief. If you're the destitute person just handed something for nothing, hero.
- Topic: Darth Vader's a hero, not a villain.

- My response: He's a villain that had a redemption arc, that's not the same thing as a straight up hero.
- Topic: Being famous is actually not great.
- My response: Don't have that problem, but it sounds more annoying than fun or flattering.
- Topic: Superheroes should have to pay for the damage they cause.
- My response: No. (One of my characters answered this in more detail.) Who gets to source the blame? Do heroes get credit for things they save? What if they choose not to get involved so they don't get blamed and charged?

There are Good Samaritan laws in place in most jurisdictions to protect people from this idea in a more realistic context.

- Topic: Living under the sea is better than space.
- My response: Neither are making real great strides in the PR department. In both places, you need food, air supply and purification, pressurization, etc. At that point, it's probably no different, except under the sea probably doesn't have gravity issues.
- Topic: Skirts are more comfortable than pants.
- My response: I guess. They tend to be lighter overall. I don't like them, but like pants, there's probably some variation in terms of comfort.

Takeaways:
- Staying in can be fun.
- Fame may not be all it's purported to be.

Chapter 49:
Episode 169 – General Opinion: Alternate Lunches

Introduction:

Dear Reader,

I found this article on a random page for MSN. It brings up an interesting issue. I'll see if I can find some of the responses to the original article.

~Ann

Source: "Inmates have it better": Tennessee School district slammed for giving alternate meals to kids behind on payments. Story by Sky Palma; 8/1/23

The title pretty much has everything you need to know.

What you should probably also know is nearly every public school I've ever heard of likely has a similar policy. It's being cast in a needlessly negative light and put before a public who generally just likes to shoot their mouths off.

The controversial policy:

Students whose lunch accounts are in the red can only charge (as in buy on credit) two lunches. After that, the kid is given either peanut butter or a cheese sandwich and milk until the balance is paid.

The school put it on their Facebook page (probably mistake #1). One commenter pointed out that inmates have it better than the kids. The person also decried the public shaming of kids for what their parents do.

Students received free lunches during the Covid-19 Pandemic, but now paid lunches are back.

The county has $29,000 in outstanding balances from last year.

Random comments:

- There are still free and reduced lunches for those who financially qualify.
- Free isn't free. In a different MSN article from (8/2/23) Clark County School District in Las Vegas Nevada is happy to declare that the school lunches are free for all students this year. A little later in the article, it says that it's funded by the National School Lunch Program (fed government).
- Please note: The school district isn't going to let a kid go hungry, but they also need to pay for the food that they give to the kids. Peanut butter sandwiches are a lot cheaper than chicken wraps with fresh vegetables.
- The inmates probably do have it better, but that's a matter of them being complete guests of the state rather than being there for education. I'm sure if you did a survey of prisons, someone there would also have an issue with what's served.

- I'd be willing to bet that the same people screaming about the injustice of an alternate meal would be the first to sit down and shut up if they had to have higher taxes to fund better free meals for other people's kids.
- An alternate meal is not really meant to be a long-term thing. It's meant to be a reminder to get the balances to a point where they're not in the red. That is a parent responsibility, not a problem that should rest with the school.
- Believe it or not there are articles that will yammer on and on at you about the stats surrounding school lunches. (schoolnutrition.org)
- California and Maine have dedicated state funding to keeping school meals free for everybody. High poverty areas have other federal programs they can utilize to keep meals free. Free and reduced is available in most districts. Everybody else has to pay for the school meals.
- The food isn't the only problem some of these programs face. Supply shortages and staff shortages are also problems that can arise. The money paid for school meals isn't just for profit, it's used to pay for the food and staff and such.
- It's not public shaming. Kids will find a way to know where the class divides are anyway. If a kid brought a lunch every day that's basic PB&J, someone would pick up on it.
- In most cases, kids don't have money except for what their parents allot them, so anything that involves money is going to be out of their control.
- Being able to charge two meals means the parents have/had two days to get their crap together and pay the bill. If they legitimately can't pay the bill, they have an uncomfortable conversation with the right office people and get on the list for free or reduced lunches.

- $29,000 sounds like a lot to me, but I don't know how many kids this district is serving. The debt has to be covered somehow. I imagine, the district would like to avoid a similar shortcoming in that portion of their budge this year.
- At my current district, I believe it can be done online with a credit card.
- Schools spend a lot of stupid money. Money gets earmarked for certain things.
- Pretty sure my current district also has a similar policy in place. I don't know what's part of the alternate meal, but having such a thing is not an unreasonable solution. In many cases, it's likely an "I forgot to put money on the account" situation over and "I can't pay" situation.
- Giving people an unlimited number of normal meals on credit or IOU would provide 0 incentive for them to fix the balance.
- There's always going to be a difference in who has how much.

Takeaways:
- Free isn't free.
- Alternate meals don't kick in unless the meal fund is somewhere in the red. In this case, two meals beyond that point.
- A school won't let your kid starve, but they're also not obligated to give them the top-tier menu items.

Chapter 50:
Episode 170 – General Opinion: Rewarding Bad Behavior is Problematic

Introduction:
We chuckle at the idea of rewarding bad behavior, but it happens.

"Dear Admin: Let This Be the Year We Stop Rewarding Bad Behavior"
Original Article by Angela Barton for Bored Teachers

Sample instances of kids being rewarded for bad behavior:
- A principal took kids to McDonald's.
- Kids come back saying "that was fun."
- Kid watched TV on the admin's iPad after being sent there for throwing a chair.
- Kid threw strawberries at another child who was allergic to them. He was chosen as Student of the Week. Woman who reported the incident ... her kid had to write a congratulatory letter to this little jerk.

- Kid got suspended. Mom bought him some new sneakers. (Not an admin thing, but still a reward for bad behavior.)

My response to those examples:
- McDonald's – yikes. I'd be terrified for multiple reasons. First, the parents could pitch a fit. Second, the liabilities of taking a kid in your personal vehicle and driving them off campus are nauseating. (I know sometimes you do what you gotta do like drive kids for sports, but usually, there are specific permissions involved.)
- Fun – should never be the reaction when being sent down for disciplinary purposes.
- Watching TV – I get the idea of wanting to calm the kid, but that's not a great precedent to set. It's not fair to every kid doing what they're supposed to.
- Student of the Week – The idea of compulsory letters is skivvy to me. Also, I can see it happening because the person who recommended the child may not have known about the incident. Rumors get around, but it is possible for a different teacher to pick the child even though he misbehaves elsewhere.
- Sneakers for suspension – Dumb. There's a difference between there-there and teaching kids that their hissy fits will bring attention and good things.

What's the harm? (according to the article ...)
- Undermines teacher's authority.
- Destroys the admin/teacher relationship.
- Tanks morale.

What should admin do? (according to the article ...)
- Build positive relationships with students before it comes to disciplinary actions.
- More help (counselors, aides, behavioral interventionists).

Have I seen this?

- Yes. My boss has a bowl of candy on her desk, and there are definitely times kids come back with candy.
- Though I don't have any specific stories like the article covered, I do know there's a general lack of respect for some of the admin. The kids pick up on the fact that little to nothing will happen. They'll sit in detention. That's about it.
- Sometimes, when kids are suspended for drugs, one wonders if we're not doing them a disservice by leaving them home, likely unsupervised.

Why does it happen?

- Because few people want to be seen as the bad guy.
- It's hard to discipline people. It makes you feel bad.
- It's the easy road.
- The kid is going to immediately show you a good attitude, so it's a false sense of I fixed the problem.
- People have this twisted idea that discipline will break children. It won't. Boundaries are a huge part of life. One needs to learn how to operate within acceptable boundaries.

What can be done?

- Admin need to do their actual jobs, not make themselves feel better.
- It's tough. I get that. But that's why they make twice as much as teachers, sometimes more. Earn it. Own it. Congrats, you get to be the bad guy from time to time.
- Tough love. Kids should know we care about them and want to hear them out on why they're doing whatever they're doing wrong. But they should still walk away from the conversation thinking *I done messed up and need to do better*.

- Not much to be done about crappy parenting. They fall into the same holes. They don't want to deal with constant conflict, so surrendering ground is the easier path.

Takeaways:

- Discipline should not be a joy for children. (Not in the moment anyway.)
- Admin need to own this part of their job.
- Teachers too need to break the cycle of rewarding crappy behavior.

Chapter 51:
Episode 171 – Back to School Musings

Introduction:

It's a new school year, and I'm still getting used to my schedule.

My school has a rolling 4-day cycle, so it's hard to tell much about what the year will look like.

There are things I like about the beginning of the year in general.

- There's a honeymoon period where the students are too shy to act out much.
- It's nice to see new faces and do the introduction stuff.
- You can start fresh.
- You get to see kids in other contexts. Everybody (well, mostly everybody) has moved up a year. Your former students will say hi in the hallways. You can have a nice conversation with them outside the confines of your classroom.
- You get to see how much kids have grown up over the summer.

Things I don't love about the beginning of the year in general.

- I don't know their faces and names. It can take a few weeks, especially with a rolling cycle, because you don't see the kids every day. The not knowing part isn't nice.
- If one loves something about their previous year's schedule, it becomes a nice memory at this point. (Change in general isn't my favorite thing.)
- Have to re-establish routines. I am in a science classroom, so I get to convince a new batch of students that they shouldn't get in the habit of chewing gum in class.
- Lines of communication need to be re-established.
- It's a new school year. It's another reminder that time flies very fast, and I'm not getting younger.

Nice things about the 23-24 school year:

- My schedule is really nice this year. I have two easy days and two hard days. Doing this from one of the easy days.
- On an easy day, I'll have two classes. On a hard day, I'll have all four classes. But even then, the way it works out, I do still get breaks.
- I have one level to teach. I have four sections, but they are all the same class. This saves me a LOT of time in terms of prep. That's why I've always wondered how my friends with multiple preps do it. Even if you have one section of something, you need to have a lesson plan for it. (I've had friends who have had up to 5 preps/classes to teach.)

Neutral:

- I have lab every day. That's weird. Usually, I get no labs some days and double lab once a cycle. I guess it's a good thing because it lets me spread out lab days if I want to. Basically, the lesson plan for the easy days is the same.
- I have a cafeteria duty every day.

- I have one class in a different room. That's strange because I sometimes have to go from one place to another. It's fine. I've done it before. (With space being limited, some teachers get bounced from class to class.) It's a little strange working from someone else's room. It can be difficult because usually, I have a lot of extra supplies in my normal desk. (Like graph paper. Luckily, the room I was moved to is very close to my normal room, and I can duck in if I need to grab something quickly.)

Forecast:

- So far, it looks like this year is going to be a good one in terms of students. The class size has a lot to do with this. Small classes means kids can get more directly help from me.

Takeaways:

- Enjoy each part of the year.
- Don't rush into the next thing and the next thing. Life will move at its own pace.

Chapter 52:
Episode 172 – Picture Day is Chaos in the Media Center

Introduction:
This year, I have a media center study hall. It's all seniors though, and they don't have to show up for it, so when it falls first block, they usually don't show up. So, I get to sit in the media center for an hour.

It's usually quite peaceful. Except on Picture Day.

Nice things about Picture Day:
- Some students dress decently. – Most are just in their normal grungy T-shirt and shorts or pajama pants, but some do make an effort to look decent. It's nice to see.
- It's a change of pace.

Setup:
- Looks like they have two people taking pictures.
- Not sure if I'd like that job.

- You have to make adjustments to each person to make sure their head is tilted the correct way and their feet are positioned right.
- It's a lot of repetition on the part of the person taking the pictures.
- They had to clear out some desks/chairs to make way for the background screens and giant lights.

Chaotic things about Picture Day:

- The students are supposed to go during their Physical Education or Health class. (I think the students get three marking period of PE and 1 of Health and it rotates through so everybody can get Health without creating massively huge classes.)
- With our rolling cycle, there are four morning and four afternoon periods. One drops in the morning and one drops in the afternoon every day because there are only three morning and three afternoon blocks. So, at least one period of morning and afternoon PE classes don't meet today. Those students were told to go before school or at lunch or after school.
- Result: Media Center is packed.
- I think one of the gym teachers came in with his class, took one look, and turned them right back around.
- The Media Center (what used to be the library) is also where the kids come to get loaner chromebooks.

Side note: Students are really hard on chromebooks. You'd think they'd be more cautious with them so they didn't have to bother getting temp equipment they have to return by the end of the day. (Then again, some do love the excuse to leave class.)

- Boom then bust. There must have been 100 kids in here this morning. Now there's practically nobody. The PE class will be back, but right now, it's a ghost town.

- It can get crazy with the morning people because you get kids in multiple classes. When there's a PE class, they will at least have the advantage of being all in the same class.
- Oohh, one kid slipped in between chaos and PE classes. Good for him.
- Getting the nameplates can be nuts because they are alphabetical by grade.
- It's hurry up and wait.
- Two gym classes are in here currently, so there are juniors and sophomores present.

Random musings:

- I'm surprised class pictures are still done this way. I mean they don't have to go into a room and develop film or anything, but video is so prevalent, I'm not sure why it's not a thing to have the kids record short videos.
- It would be a pain to control that and you'd probably have to bleep out a bunch, but it would be interesting.
- I've never been super fond of yearbooks. I am surprised there isn't an electronic version with videos. Would be an editing nightmare, but doable.
- Used to buy a yearbook every year, but then I changed schools and never looked at them anyway. Kind of a waste of money.

Procedure:

- The kids need to pick up a slip of paper that has their name and grade on it. I think it has a QR code on it.
- I think they take a picture of the slip then the kid so that the information is correct.
- Once they have the correct slip, they have to wait in line for the two people taking pictures. Each kid can take 30 s to a minute, so when you need to get through a class of 50, that can take a while.

Side notes on dress code:

- There is a dress code, but it's not enforced super well.
- Uniforms aren't a thing in most U.S. schools. (I'm reading these articles about fuss over shoes in England.) People will always find a way to stand out.

Takeaways:

- Do your best to look decent when you're out in public.
- Get used to standing in line for Picture Day.

Chapter 53:
Episode 173 – Someone on Staff Freaked Out and it Scared Us

Introduction:

Dear Ann,

We had an incident with a custodian today. Normally, he's very affable, but today, he freaked out.

My colleague and I had switched out the table in the copy room because it was flimsy. We didn't want the printer to break.

Part of the freakout involved him dragging desks down a hallway, screaming profanities, trashing my colleague's project (which scared her).

When the head custodian was contacted, things got worse, not better.

We told our side of the story to the principal and assistant principal, but we're worried this might come back to us in terms of our rooms not getting cared for or something like this happening in front of children.

VP said the man would have to apologize.

This is a Christian school and usually staff and teachers are very nice.

What should I do?

~Concerned Christian Teacher

Responses from others:
- At a Christian school, use of profanity has been grounds for dismissal. I too would be worried of future incidents.
- I'm surprised that more people aren't willing to extend this man grace. If you're truly afraid, get a restraining order.
- Document what happened and pray.
- Maybe investigate if there's a medical issue. That would be a matter for the man's family.
- Being a custodian is hard and thankless. Maybe you should apologize for moving stuff.
- Re: apology to custodian. What? This is exactly what's wrong with this country. We should not expect victims to apologize. Nor should we not be holding people accountable for their actions. Pray for this man, certainly!
- Multiple instances of he should be fired.
- Don't worry about the room. That's small compared to the rest.

My response:
Dear Concerned Christian Teacher,

I'm not sure there's much you can do besides tell your VP and Principal. It sounds like things have already proceeded.

General points:
- Every school has a policy on stuff like this (the profanity

anyway). It might go against a code of conduct. I'm curious as to how the situation got worse when the head custodian was contacted.

- The behavior does sound disturbing, but you don't really have to worry about whether or not it's a termination sort of offense.
- Forced apologies aren't always the best thing.
- I wouldn't worry about your room.
- If it bothers you, I'd suggest reaching out to hear this man's side of the story. You don't have to play peacemaker here, but it might help. You don't have to worry about what consequences do or do not befall him. That's out of your sphere of influence.
- It's quite possible the whole thing gets brushed under a rug somewhere. Be ready to accept that outcome. Much as we would like there to be consequences for actions. There should also be an investigation of mitigating circumstances. Even a medical reason would not totally absolve the behavior though. That's part of the problem with schools in general. Mostly as it applies to student behavior.
- Being a custodian can be hard, thankless work, but that doesn't seem to be the main issue here.

Advice for what to do:
- I'd concentrate on comforting your colleague. Help her with the project that got wrecked. See if she's okay now that some time has passed. Witnessing someone losing it can be frightening.
- If you wish, reach out and see what's up with the custodian as well. If the behavior is out of character, there's got to be some reason. Was it just a straw that broke the camel sort of situation or was there some other reason?

- I don't you owe any apologies, but I also wouldn't hold my breath to receive a forced one from him.
- Don't worry about retaliation. The job may or may not be done to its fullest, but that has little to do with you. Few people have the energy to be that passive-aggressive and vindictive.

Takeaways:

- Cautiously move on.
- Pray over the situation.
- Being kind and understanding is not always synonymous with letting people walk all over you.

Chapter 54:
Episode 174 – General Opinion: The Case of Good Little Teacher vs. Adult Content Worker

Introduction:

How much should one's private life be under a microscope if they are a teacher?

That's the question that has popped up.

Once again OnlyFans is in the spotlight (but not really). It's just a means to an end.

The Story: Teacher's OnlyFans account gets her put on leave.
Source: Original article by Devan Markham for pix11.com. Posted on October 2, 2023 and updated on the 3rd.

The details: (are kind of scant)

- A high school teacher got put on leave after someone discovered she was performing pornographic stuff for an OnlyFans account.

- She teaches English.
- Lady says her teaching days are over. (She doesn't seem broken up about it.)
- She makes $42,000 a year as a teacher. (Yikes, that's low. I don't know how that compares to the cost of living, but I made more than that as a first-year teacher with a Master's degree.)
- She absolutely knew the risks. She did it anyway to the tune of $8K-$10K a month. (That's a lot of money, but like anything, it won't last forever.)
- She doesn't think sex work should be shameful.
- What is shameful is the way teachers are underpaid.

My response to the story:
Practical points:

- Lady doesn't seem broken up about it.
- Lady's salary of $42K a year. – Yikes, that's low. I don't know how that compares to the cost of living, but I made more than that as a first-year teacher with a Master's degree.
- $8K to $10K extra is a lot of money, but like anything, it won't last forever. I doubt it's taxed, so that will be something for her to consider. As a business, she'll have to save for the future because there's no retirement plan.
- It's also volatile. OnlyFans as of August was going to ban explicit content. No more sex stuff, bye bye very large income. They did reverse that call, but the point remains that someone may be betting a lot on a single basket where they've piled all their eggs.
- As with much of the "entertainment" business, there's a ticking clock attached to how long someone's body is going to cooperate.

- Sex work not being shameful – debatable. I suppose that depends on your moral upbringing. From my personal background, yeah, that's a no-no.
- The whole thing about OnlyFans being a hub and safe place to sell explicit content is an entirely separate debate.
- Teachers being underpaid – Agreed. People don't understand what the job entails. They think anybody can do it, so it's not worth a lot. Glorified babysitting. Some days are. You know what days those are? State testing days of which there are many. Whose fault is that? Likely a system run by so and sos who haven't spent a day in a classroom ever. But I digress.

Moral musings:

- Through the moral lens: Is sex work shameful? Yup. Has that stopped the world's oldest profession from existing? Nope. Is the existence of this a problem? Yes, it's a sign of how sinful the world is. Sin is quite literally praised as good.
- Without the benefit of definite morals (more of a do-as-you-will philosophy): Is sex work shameful? No. The worlds oldest profession exists to serve a need. As long as everybody's consenting adults, no harm, no foul. Is the existence of things like OnlyFans to support this bad? No. On the contrary, it provides a safe haven for those who wish to sell their wares while maintaining some semblance of distance. (This only holds true if you're willing to buy that teachers should NOT be held to a higher moral standard. In which case, why bother with fingerprint checks? Without a moral compass, hire anybody off the street. Should be safe enough.)
- Should be pretty clear which camp I fall into. But from a secular standpoint. She hasn't done anything illegal.

- I liken this to something like drinking alcohol. It's legal for adults but deemed too risky for children. Conceptually, an adult should be able to drink at home/ on their own time. By the same token an adult should also be able to do what they will (that isn't illegal) on their own time. However, school should never come up and this should never come up at school. Complete separation.

- It's a very, very gray area. For better or worse, double standards exist. Kids look up to their teachers in many cases. It's murky business when something like this could influence a kid to follow in her footsteps while still being underaged. So, the key question is: how much weight do you place on moral character?

- For a public school, I think the answer would be different than a private, religion-based school. Given the code of conduct at many private schools, this would be grounds for dismissal.

Disclaimer: I don't work for the company. I do have an account which I opened exactly once to see what a friend was doing. It does not hide what it is.

- What's so appealing about OnlyFans? It's a transactional site. For a price, people can unlock exclusive content. I think there's even a way for a person to pay more to get the account holder to do something specific for them. That's some heady power if you're into the manipulation of other humans.

- Even from a secular standpoint, I'm not a fan of the purposeful objectification of one's body. It has the potential to set up both unrealistic expectations and the idea that money can buy anything.

Suggestion:

- Lady should quit teaching altogether and enjoy her new, likely very brief but lucrative new career. (As long as her husband is okay with it. He seemed to be.) She's never going to get everybody to be okay with her double life. True enough, same could be said for most second careers. That's why writers who wander to the dark and depraved side tend to use pen names if they teach.
- She doesn't seem broken up about leaving teaching.
- She shouldn't have money problems for a while at least.
- I'm simultaneously on the side of: eeeeep, she shouldn't have done that because it's morally questionable and it's none of their (the school's) business. Who the heck outted her anyway? What the heck were they doing following someone they know is a teacher they know on that site?

Takeaways:

- Fair or not, double standards exist for teachers.
- I vote separation of home and school life if you want to wander the dark side of adult only stuffs. (To be fair, she didn't bring it up. Others brought it up for her.)
- Have some self-respect people. (Others will argue that the money being stellar makes up for it. I haven't the time to argue with you here. But do leave me some comments, we'll have a civilized adult conversation.)

Chapter 55:
Episode 175 – General Opinion: Doing the Kids' Homework for them?

Introduction:
*Spoiler alert: Don't.

We could probably do many discussions concerning homework. On the whole, this is NOT about the existence of homework as a thing.

It's about what one woman says she does and that is the homework that should be done by her children.

Source: Shania Obrien for Daily Mail Australia; from October 8, 2023, updated on the 9th.

The story details:
- A mother who doesn't want her kids to have stress concerning homework does it for them.
- The internet has largely called her a bad mother for encouraging her kids to be lazy. (Others called it genius.)
- She wants to raise kids that are honest and strong.

- Some of the projects are too hard for the kids.
- She "tries" not to baby them.
- Others do the same.

The internet says:
- Glad I'm not the only one.
- Work with your kids.
- Not having homework was detrimental to one lady's kids.
- My kid just doesn't do the homework.
- Home is a homework free zone. Reading is acceptable but that's it.
- Congrats on setting those kids up for failure.
- Not exactly doing them a favor.
- Why are kids given homework anyway?
- Is she gonna take their exams too?
- Real problem is encouraging ignorance. No wonder she finds the assignments *too hard* for them.
- Your kid is overscheduled.
- You are the source of this useless generation.
- Hope the kids don't mind getting homework wrong because she doesn't seem like the sharpest knife.

The Key Questions:
- What is this teaching the kids?
- Is this a good idea?
- Is this coddling?
- Is this encouraging laziness?

My response to the story:
- I'd vote just don't do the homework over doing it for the kids.
- It's too small a sample size to see if this would harm most people. Honestly, we won't know for another 5-10 years if

it's harmful. And if it turns out to be harmful, it's way too late.

- Is it coddling? Heck, yes.
- Is it encouraging laziness? Not sure. It is reinforcing the idea that mom will do everything for you for ever and always. (This is going to be followed 20 years down the line with the article: why are my kids living in my basement instead of being fully functioning adults.)
- Is this a good idea? Not really, no.
- What is it teaching the kids? Deception. Cheating. Claiming work that isn't your own. Clearly, this mother is okay with that, but most people aren't okay with people claiming their work as their own. We may think cheating in school is harmless, but the problem kicks in when people don't confine the bad behavior to the school setting. It bleeds over into work and life. Committed relationships have a hard enough time flourishing without a very fluid mindset on getting what you want by any means necessary.

Why is homework given? Some random points:

- Sometimes, it counts as part of the grade. Oh, we could spend days talking about grading systems.
- Mostly, it's extra practice for stuff that would be on exams.
- Elementary grades are foundational. There are helpful things like use this vocabulary word in a sentence. Can it be tedious? Sure, but the context helps.
- What is homework? Usually, it's practice.
- Sports/exercise analogy – Practice can be difficult, tiring, and stressful, but if you want to perform well in the game itself, you need to do hard things ahead of time. You need to do them a lot, until that thing/ action becomes second nature. (There are people who skip practices because "they

don't matter" then wonder why they suck during the game. Well, gee, there's a tough one. Same principle is in play.)

- Homework in my class is largely optional. It's simply more of what they can expect to see on a test. If doing one problem is enough, great. If they need to do the whole thing and still ask for more help, also fine. But having someone else do the work for them is going to teach them all the wrong lessons.

What should parents do?

- Well, absolutely not this.
- Instead, work with the child, even if you can't finish the whole thing because it's slower.
- Bike riding analogy – You can't learn how to bike ride if your mom won't let you on the bike. You need training wheels, patience, and the lessons learned from taking a tumble or two.

Why not?

- This is exactly the sort of parent who is going to later complain about the educational system failing her child in the broader sense of the word (meaning they're not prepared to face life).
- I think the deception bothers me more than the coddling.
- If you want to do their work for them, cut out the middleman and homeschool. Then you can give them as much or little help as you want. The only person you'll be fooling or deluding then is you.
- It's a bad precedent to set. (Does your kid know what precedent is? Probably not if you didn't give them the room to grow.) You will eventually reach a point when the work of 3 people will become too much (because it's designed for 3 people).

- Much as you want to bubble-wrap your kid, you aren't helping them by reinforcing learned helplessness.
- What is learned helplessness? They come to believe "this is too difficult" for them, so they don't try. Because they don't try, they fail.

Takeaways:

- People do indeed have a right to be wrong. But this should also disqualify them from complaining later when school is a very large struggle for their kids in the future.
- Helping is very different than doing something for someone else.
- Homework is practice. In not letting your kid do homework, you could be denying them the much-needed practice.

Chapter 56:
Episode 176 – Special Guest:
90's Teacher

Introduction:
It's hard to imagine how much the education system has changed over the years. There are people teaching at all levels who weren't even born during the 90's.

What would you like me to call you?
90's Teacher.

Me: Offbeat. I like it.

How many years did you teach?
90's Teacher: 8 years in a public school. I'm still teaching music privately (past 15 years).

Did you have a different career?
90's Teacher: Yes, right out of college I worked in retail management for 9 months before realizing that was not the career for me.

Me: Retail anything sounds really hard.

Did you have friends in high school?
90's Teacher: Yes.

Did you get close to any teachers when you were a student?
90's Teacher: On a "real" basis, not really. In my mind, a few teachers were my first crushes. I was a shy, good girl and this felt like a safe way to deal with all the overwhelming emotions of adolescence.

Why did you choose teaching?
90's Teacher: My dad was a teacher.

Growing up, I did very well in school and my parents encouraged me to pursue a field where intelligence was valued—medicine, law, etc. Unfortunately, none of those things appealed to me. I switched majors all the time in college, ending up with a retail degree which was a bad idea.

I had always liked kids, liked school, and was familiar with "teacher life" since my dad was one. So, I found a program where an addition 1 year of college work could get me my teaching license, and I completed that.

How long did it take you to prep?
90's Teacher: Not sure what you mean by this.

Me: Prepare for class. A lot of teachers tend to take time outside of school to prepare lessons for their classrooms. The question is about how much time it took you (on average) to get yourself ready for class.

How do you approach prep?
90's Teacher: Same as previous question.

Me: This one has more to do with methodology. It's the how did you get ready for class question.

What kind of school did you work in?
90's Teacher: Public elementary school.

Me: Elementary school is a whole other beast than high school.

What classes did you teach?
90's Teacher: Grades 2, 3, 4, and 6 over 8 years. I wanted to work with younger kids, but usually the openings were in the older grades. I started in grade 6 and worked my way down as there were openings there each year.

Me: That's a lot of grades though I suppose throughout my career I've taught a range too.

What was the most preps you had in a year?
90's Teacher: ??
Me: This question has to do with the number of courses you teach in a year. How many things did you have to get yourself ready for in one year.

What was your favorite class to teach? Favorite topic?
90's Teacher: I loved social studies. I've always loved to travel, as well as enjoying the medieval period, etc. When I taught, in the 1990's, there was a lot of freedom to swerve from the official curriculum.

If the social studies book topics looked boring to me, I'd swap them out for a unit on medieval life, for instance. So many opportunities for things that would really excite kids with a love for learning.

Me: That sounds awesome. Yeah, they're a little more cranky about going off script these days.

What was your least favorite class to teach?
90's Teacher: Probably science. I'm not anti-science by any means, but I just hadn't taken tons of science classes in school.

I still remember weekends, that first year teaching sixth grade, when I'd be at home trying the science experiments in the book before we tried them in class. Also, trying to learn and remember the difference between types of circuits, etc., at least well enough that I could explain them to the kids.

Me: Ick. Physics. Chemistry is cool.

What is the best, worst, and most fun part of teaching?
90's Teacher:
- Best – the kids individually and the opportunity to creatively share fun information with them.
- Worst – at least with sixth graders, it was often the kids as a group (hormones were kicking in and this could result in some anti-authority behavior).
- Most fun – I loved creating units we'd do in the classroom that would bring learning alive.

Second graders going out on the playground to reenact Columbus's voyage on Columbus Day.

Learning about "mad" King Ludwig and his castles in Germany, then having the kids design and create their own castles.

Learning about medieval times and then having one day be a "day in the monastery" complete with eating rye bread, hearing cassette tapes of chanting, and "illuminating" beautiful letters.

Creating a "wall" through the center of the classroom which we left there for half the day, then "tore it down" to feel a bit of what Germans might have felt when their actual wall came down. SO many memories like this with "my kids."

Me: Wow. Haven't touched a cassette tape in decades. Yikes!

Do you have any advice for new teachers?

90's Teacher: It varies so much. It's been 27 years since I've taught in public schools, and a lot depends on specific situations. Overall, I feel like it's very important for elementary teachers to have a real love of kids. (I've seen many teachers who didn't even seem to like kids much, which usually didn't turn out too well.)

Also, although people can't do much about this, I feel it's great when a teacher can be intelligent. I remember many "dumb" teachers I had in school. They didn't inspire me, and I became so bored in their classes.

It's unfortunate that education programs often seem to attract those of lesser ability. And I fully admit that teacher education programs in college are not difficult; this is probably why.

Me: Yeah, my Masters program (after an undergrad in a science) was a cakewalk.

What do you think kids need to succeed at school?

90's Teacher: A good attitude and the ability to work hard and stick to things. Give me a kid who is persistent and has a good attitude any day over a smart kid who's a slacker and has a bad attitude.

Were you involved in any extracurriculars as a teacher?

90's Teacher: Yes, "coach" of Battle of the Books.

Me: I'd never heard of that. It's a reading incentive program. When I was a kid, I read books for pizza.

When do you think the emphasis on grades kicks in?

90's Teacher: In elementary, "real" grades including ones in social studies and science, begin. Honestly, a lot of the answer to this depends on the individual family and how much they value education/learning/grades/achievement.

How did the pandemic affect teaching?

90's Teacher: I would NOT have wanted to teach during the pandemic.

Even teaching music in my home, it was not great as I was dealing with 20 different kids/families, each of whom had their own thoughts on masking, whether or not in-person was safe, etc.

I did several months of Zoom music teaching, and for most of the kids I'd say they progressed barely if at all. The sound quality was poor. I think we'll be seeing the effects of a year or two "off" from education for decades to come with a generation of kids whose education was affected by the pandemic.

Thanks! This was fun.

Me: My pleasure. Thank you for sharing your experiences. I have enjoyed learning about what teaching was like in the 90's.

Chapter 57:
Episode 177 – Special Guest: Lisa
Special Ed Teacher, Editor, Organizer

Introduction:

Been a while. Had some health stuff catch up to me, but I'm ready to jump back into this series.

First up, let's do a traditional interview.

What would you like to be called throughout the interview?

I'm just called Lisa.

Me: That works.

What kind of school did you attend? Did you enjoy school?

Lisa: I went through a typical public school system for K-12. I always more or less liked school more. Some years were better than others. I wasn't a fan of those middle school years. After high school, I went to college and then got my master's in education.

What kind of training did you do for your job?

Lisa: I've had a variety of jobs, but I went through formal training to be a teacher. I never did official student teaching (I kind of fell into a job and "sort of" learned there), but I had a couple of practicums that required me to go into classrooms here and there. I always worked with kids—babysitting, camp counselor, etc.—so that's probably where the bulk of my training came in.

What do you know now that you wish you knew back before you were preparing for your career?

Lisa: I think what I most wish I knew—and what I'd like to tell younger people now—is that you don't have to know all the answers at 18, or really ever, to what you want to do when you grow up.

Life is a fluid journey, and we learn as we go where our interests and skill sets fall. I realized after ten plus years into being a special education teacher that teaching large groups really isn't my thing. I love 1:1 teaching, and I like to teach in other capacities other than the classroom. For a while, I regretted spending time and resources on going to school to become a teacher, but now I see I can use that knowledge in other ways.

Did you always know what you wanted to do? How old were you when that realization hit? In other words, how did you end up with the job you have/are going to talk about?

Lisa: When I was little, I wanted to be a teacher, and I wanted to be an author. At some point, I randomly wanted to be an interior decorator. Right now, I do each of these in some capacity.

As I mentioned, although I went to school to be a secondary special education teacher, I left the classroom eleven years ago, right before I had kids. I started a tutoring business during my last year of teaching. I had a bunch of adult students looking for help with writing, and that somehow segued into my becoming an editor.

What other jobs did you hold before this?

Lisa:

- Babysitter
- Camp counselor
- Food services in college
- Retail (that didn't last too long)
- Special education paraprofessional
- Professional home organizer

Please describe your job. What do you do?

Lisa: I split my time between teaching reading, mostly virtually, to students with dyslexia and learning disabilities and working as a freelance editor. I'd like to say that I'm a fledgling author, and I also still do some home organizing here and there.

To be honest, the organizing is my favorite of my jobs, but if I have to decide between putting my time and resources into really building a professional organizing business or an author business, I choose the writing. I've learned that trying to chase all the rabbits keeps me at a standstill.

Is this your dream job?

Lisa: My ultimate dream job would be splitting my time between professional organizing and writing. People (myself included) feel so much better after they've decluttered and have space to breathe. It's a way of giving back while doing something I'm passionate about. But I also do love working with kids, as well as adults and helping them gain confidence in reading.

Right now, both my teaching job and editing job are virtual, and the editing is extremely flexible I really can't complain. I'd have to say that I do have a dream job because I can see my kids off to school in the morning, reheat my coffee all day long, sneak in a run or load of laundry, and talk to my husband—who also works from home—throughout the day.

Me: That's nice. Guess you have to stay organized to separate work and personal space.

What equipment/stuff do you need to do your job?

Lisa: I need the internet to work. For tutoring, I have a set of materials and a doc camera, so it almost seems like I'm there with the kiddos. I need lots of sticky notes and planners to keep track of what I'm trying to do. I plunk myself at the high-top table by the window where I can look out into the backyard and woods and walk right to the kitchen get more caffeine when I need it.

Me: I've done a little bit of virtual tutoring. It went fine. It's a better commute than in person. Tutoring is decent money when one can get jobs. I don't really seek them out though. I've always got more stuff to do.

Where do you fit in the organizational system? (boss, sole employee, owner, worker, employee, etc.)

Lisa: I'm mostly my own boss right now, but as part of my job, I am currently working as an independent contractor for a multi-sensory reading organization.

What was the hiring process like?

Lisa: Usually, I talk with a client or have a video chat, allowing the client to get to know me, ask questions about services, and see if it's a good fit. If I'm interviewing to be an independent contractor with an organization, virtual Zoom interviews still seem to be the norm. Sometimes there's a second interview involved with those.

Me: Never thought about doing a pre-meeting. Usually, it's just described on my website. Most of the tutoring stuff is direct referral from a friend. I have a colleague who does over 20 hours of tutoring some weeks. That's a lot of tutoring. He does a lot more than just chemistry though. He does ACT/SAT prep, which is very much in demand in the area where we work.

If your job involves a product/creative thing, tell us about 1 or 2 of your favorite projects. Why is it meaningful to you?

Lisa: I use a structured reading program, which allows for some creativity, just enough that I don't go down rabbit holes, a tendency I had when I was developing all curriculum. I actually love curriculum design, but I could easily get overwhelmed with all the choices. Now, I use a couple of websites to make some real quick reading games to hold engagement, but I save most of my creativity for my own writing projects. This works for me!

Why do you do what you do?

Lisa: I like to help people, and I like to create. My work involves opportunities for both.

Do you like your job?

Lisa: I really do!

What do you consider your greatest job triumph?

Lisa: When a client sees results. I had an 8-year-old boy tell me a few weeks ago that he had never been able to spell a word before, but that during our session he spelled six words. He was so proud of himself. That carried me for a little while.

Me: That's a great feeling. Ha, my students go from grumbling and complaining to cursing to that ah-ha, well, this isn't so bad. And yes, no matter what age they are, that moment of triumph is special.

What do you like about your job?

Lisa: I like helping people, and I like the flexibility. I've learned that I'm much more of a 1:1 person than a person who leads big groups – like whole classrooms.

What is difficult about your job?

Lisa: Sometimes I have kids, on the other hand, who use avoidance techniques.

What's ugly or messy (less fun) about your job? (you can interpret those words any way you like)

Lisa: Being an entrepreneur means marketing, and I hate marketing.

I rely too much on putting my names and services on platforms and hoping someone will reach out. This is something in which I need to gain confidence in any of the jobs I do. I can only get so far if I'm afraid to promote. It's for this reason that I like that I work very part time for an agency. That way, I know for at least a little bit that someone will find my clients for me.

Me: Yup. Marketing is tough.

If you didn't need to work for the money, would you still hold the same job?

Lisa: I would. I would focus more on the organizing and writing / author aspects of my job, but I would still want to teach and edit too.

What advice do you have for those considering your career? (Any training, tips, hints, tricks?)

Lisa: I'm just going to speak for being your own boss in general. I feel that if you want to, there's a way.

What life lessons has your job taught you?

Lisa: Simple is better and progress over perfection.

What's the best/worst/funniest thing to happen in your life thus far?

Lisa: The best thing is meeting my husband and starting my family. Being a mom is actually my favorite job (although ask me again when my kid gets through this tween thing!)

What would make your life even better?

Lisa: If things were simpler. My word for January and February is declutter. It's been my word forever, but I want to act on it more ruthlessly. I want to focus on what's truly important and meaningful.

Do you have any pets? (please describe)
Lisa: We have chickens, although they live outside. A puppy may be in the picture in the near future.

Me: I want a puppy interview when you get there!

Are you close with your family?
Lisa: Yes, very.

What do you do for fun?
Lisa: I love to be outdoors, go camping, hiking, running, and spending time with family.

What's a risk you took that paid off?
Lisa: When I was in my early 20s, I ran a marathon in Anchorage and booked the flight for a week after. Over the week, I met interesting people and learned to hitchhike with some other travelers.

At the end of the week, I had said goodbye to my traveler friends, and I was supposed to take 1000 or km bus ride from Whitehorse, Canada back to Anchorage. I couldn't stand the idea of being stuck in a vehicle for that distance with the windows shut, etc. I considered hitchhiking, but I hadn't yet done it on my own. Then I thought ... What if?

So, I canceled my bus, grabbed my bag, stood on the sidewalk outside of the "roadhouse" where I had been staying, and stuck out my thumb. The first person to drive by yelled at me that I had the wrong thumb out. But after that, it became the adventure of a lifetime. I met the most amazing people and saw the most amazing landscape firsthand over the next 36 hours.

Would I do it again? Never! I mean, how wrong could it have gone? My husband jokes never to tell our kids I did that. Yet, when

I'm at a decisions crossroads, I think back to that experience, how taking the crazy risk turned into such an exhilarating, life altering experience. It's one of my life's metaphors and an adventure I'll never forget.

Me: Well, I'm glad you didn't get murdered during that adventure.

What's a risk you took that burned you?
Lisa: I guess I'm lucky the one above didn't burn me. I haven't done anything too crazy that has burned me, but I have taken jobs that have burned me. I had dreams of making a difference with inner city teaching but only felt—and was maybe told—that I was failing when I didn't have the resources to truly be successful. Maybe that's why I prefer to work for myself.

Me: Oh, that is a big one. You need resources, and there's only so much you can do if people aren't willing to give you those resources.

Do you think you are successful?
Lisa: It depends on the day. Some days I feel like I've been successful and others not. I feel more successful about some things than others. I feel like I've had lots of supports in my life to help me along the way, so if I am successful, it's definitely with the help of others.

What do you do if you're stressed?
Lisa: I get outside, run, be in nature, indulge in the occasional glass of wine.

Would you call yourself a contented person?
Lisa: I don't know if I'm content, but I am blessed. I've got a lot of good in my life. However, I am a worrier, and I don't tend to be content for long periods of time. I can be content in a moment, like feeling my little girl's hand in mine or lying on the couch listening to the rain.

What are your thoughts on the meaning of life?

Lisa: In the end, I think it's all about the people and relationships. That being said, I'm not the greatest at keeping in touch with people, making phone calls, etc. I need to be better.

Nobody works in a void. Who or what do you work for?

Lisa: I work for my clients. I'd like to continue to try to build a writing career, but I need to also work with people.

Would you survive in an apocalypse? Why or why not?

Lisa: Based on my ability to barely survive the toilet paper crisis during covid, probably not!

In all seriousness, though, I'm a minimalist at heart. Less is always best for me. Plus, I simply don't have survival skills.

Me: True. That was a weird time.

What animal do you most relate to?

Lisa: Eagles, dogs, and frogs.

Me: Interesting. Those are very different animals, but maybe that's what fits. You also do a lot and have many roles.

Do you like to exercise or play sports?

Lisa: I enjoy running and hiking.

Do you consider yourself a fan of something? If so, what?

Lisa: It's always hard for me to pick favorites, but I have a few. I love loose leaf pu-her tea (I could and usually do drink it all day). I love 60s and 70s music, and the band Chicago is my all-time favorite. I really enjoy the rhythm of the four seasons in New England. I like sitting outside in the with a warm jacket and a cup of coffee or a glass of wine while making dinner on Sunday night.

Pens or pencils? Do you go with whatever or a specific brand?

Lisa: I like pencils, but the design has to call to me.

What is your favorite dessert, meal, food in general?

Lisa: It's hard to pick faves, but a few of my favorite staples are Dave's Killer bread, avocados, sushi, and chili.

What is your favorite candy?

Lisa: Justin's Dark Chocolate Peanut Butter Cups.

Me: Chocolate and peanut butter in quite nice.

If you could convey just one life lesson to someone, what would it be?

Lisa: Help people whenever you can.

Additional Ques for Creatives: (Going to put this here since it's not really long enough to stand on its own and it fits here anyway.)

How do you generate leads to get new clients?

Lisa: I have a few online lead databases where I've listed my services, one of which has worked well for me. Word of mouth can be helpful too.

What's your process when you get a new job? (you can describe in general or a single project example or cover how it varies)

Lisa: It varies, depending on whether it's editing or tutoring/teaching. For my editing jobs, once the client decides to move forward, I'll draft a simple agreement about expectations, dates for completion, rates, etc. Then, we get on our way!

How important is communication?

Lisa: Communication is super important, I'll aways try to keep my editing clients up to date with how things are coming, let them know where the project stands, and keep them posted if for whatever reason we are pushing time a little. I like to try to throw in a few positive comments along the way too. Communication builds relationships.

What's the shortest/longest project you've worked on?

Lisa: I've edited a couple of quick blurbs. I've also worked on some novels for over a year, especially if the client comes back for a second round of edits.

What's your favorite/least favorite type of project to work on?

Lisa: I love editing fiction, especially romance, as well as kids' stories! I've written / edited a few wedding speeches, etc., and those have been fun too! My least favorite is probably academic writing. I've done some of those, but I worry about making APA mistakes and I don't want to accidentally do the work for them. I've pretty much stopped doing these.

On the other hand, I don't mind sitting down with a student and helping them go through the steps of composing a paper.

Do you have your own projects too? How do you balance client work with your own work?

Lisa: I have my own writing projects. The balance is tough, but I'm learning to create blocks of the day for my own writing if I want it to get done.

How do you promote your work? (there may be some overlap here)

Lisa: Right now, I only promote my work on Vella. I'm desperately trying to finish the first one (It's a complete novel that went through edits, and I'm putting the chapters on Vella as I make revision), but it's taking me so long. Once that's done, I'll figure out how to market across other platforms. I hope so anyways!

Can you describe a typical day? (I imagine it's not 9-5)

Lisa: My days tend to vary, but there's a general rhythm. I'd like to get up at 5 or earlier, but it's usually closer to 6. I oversee my tween son get off (a.k.a. try to force him to wear a jacket to the bus stop, only to discover it curled in a wad on the stairs after he's left). Then, I help my 9-year-old daughter as she goes through her fourteen-step process of getting ready for school.

After the kids leave, I do prepping for my tutoring clients and try to get in a quick run or elliptical before seeing clients. That goes till about midday. Then things start to get murky as I try to prioritize editing for clients, maybe doing my own writing, wondering what I should make for dinner, thinking about the laundry that should be put away, etc.

It's usually a combination of that for an hour or two before seeing some more clients. Once my kids get home, I may have another client or two, and then I try to spend time with them, as well as play taxi driver to their activities. Then it's dinner and an overdrawn bedtime routine. At the end of the day, I like to read some Vellas, maybe get in some writing, and spend a little time with my husband.

How do you work in breaks? (Schedule? As needed?)

Lisa: I like using the Pomodoro method. A break may be a real break, or it may be work and then a 15-minute chore. I still like doing that. At least it gets me moving. My husband works at home, so sometimes we'll just take a quick ride to Dunkins as a break. We're in a coastal town, so even just driving by the water for 5 minutes can be nice.

What's the best/worst part about being your own boss?

Lisa:
- The best part is making my own rules.
- Flexibility is a close second.

- That also could be the worst part. I enjoy creating my own structure, but prioritizing can be stressful sometimes.

Do you go to conferences? Why/why not?

Lisa: I used to go to conferences but haven't in a while.

How complicated are taxes?

Lisa: They're complicated. I leave that to my husband. Fortunately, that's his thing.

Me: If you don't have a husband who does that, just hire it out. Thanks for your time. I appreciate the chance to learn more about you.

Chapter 58:
Episode 178 – Things Teachers Sometimes Feel Guilty For (And Should NOT have to Apologize For)

Introduction:
Teaching is kind of an odd profession. Nothing in this post is surprising, but I think it's good to have it all in one place again.

Source: A Facebook post by WeAreTeachers.

Had 1.7K comments as of 2/6/24.

I will not be noting all, but there were definitely some that dominated. List and commentary may be interspersed.

The List:
- Using the restroom. – I think this is a fitting one to have first. I know I've gotten into the habit of not drinking a lot because of this. Certain days I have a lot of time, and other days, there's hardly a spare minute.
- Enjoying breaks and days off. Taking days off.
- Eating.

- Being firm but fair with expectations.
- Expecting anything from the students. High expectations for students concerning work and behavior.
- Prioritizing their own kids' health and wellbeing.
- Having a life outside of school. – Ran into his one being a writer and wanting to go to a conference when I was untenured. They said no and I had to cancel those plans or risk losing the job. They dictate everything about what you can and can't take off for. (Now, they try, but I can just do it anyway because the worst they can do is dock my pay. $300 loss is painful but not the end of the world and definitely not worth cancelling my plans.)
- Wanting a safe workplace.
- Expecting and hoping for support from school boards and administration.
- Being human. – Wasn't quite sure what this one meant, but I think it's heralding back to the days of society having very high expectations of teachers. Remember those old, old ads put in the papers outlining the expectations of the school teacher?
- A student's grades. – Oh, that one resonates. Never thought of it like that, but it's true. We are asked to defend everything we did to prevent a kid from failing, when the true reason the kid failed isn't a learning disability, it's straight, unadulterated laziness.
- Teaching. – Not sure where they're going with this one, but I think it has to do with the many other things we're asked to do besides teach curriculum stuffs.
- Prioritizing ourselves and/or our health.
- Leaving on time. (or early) – I think most of this one comes from jealousy and a misunderstanding of what it means to start school at a few minutes before 8:00 am. That means

the teacher's day often starts a half-hour to an hour before this. So, it's definitely not a 9-5 P.M. thing.

- Expecting the students to behave themselves and be respectful (not just to us, but to their peers.) – I had to tell a student today to work on his people skills. He has a habit of calling out stupid crap while I'm teaching. It's not malicious but just insults at his classmates for little mistakes or boasts about how much better he understands it or complaints about how this is stupid.
- Wanting a raise. (Wanting fair wages.) – I don't know of a single other profession where there's a new, sweeping contract that has to be renegotiated every three years.
- Wanting to feel valued.
- Personal space. – This one isn't really a problem for me, but I work with high schoolers. Mostly, one ends up yelling at them to stop touching each other.
- Telling the truth. – Ah, that is a rough one too. We're always expected to find the good and couch negatives in positives and some other BS. Nobody likes to hear that their kid is just addicted to their phone or just shy of being a completely feral human.
- Consequences to actions. – Grace is truly something misused and abused by the system.
- Boundaries.
- Advocating for students.
- Having opinions. – You really can't please everybody here. The students should feel safe enough to have opinions, but in most cases, we're supposed to hide what we feel.
- Caring.
- Respect.
- Taking a personal day.

- Getting sick. – It's difficult to take a day off. Sometimes, you just push through because it's more of a pain to get subplans together.
- Thinking school should be fun too.
- Simply teaching the lesson. – There's a high expectation for everything to be gamified these days. Using technology is good, but sometimes, a lesson is still a valuable lesson without the bells and whistles.
- Getting a pension. – It's not perfect, but it is nice if you can make it there.
- Choosing not to participate in extracurricular stuff.
- Sitting at the desk. – I forgot about this one. But I have heard it before. Get up, move around.
- Wearing jeans to work. – Each school is different when it comes to this one.
- Not being "fair" in class.
- Having to discipline a student.
- Not grading stuff at home. – I've finally reached this blissful state. But I do occasionally grade stuff at home. Normally, I can fit it into a prep period or before school or after school in those quiet moments before going home.
- Needing help. – I hadn't really thought about that, but it's true. You're expected to have all the answers, so needing help is sort of looked down upon.
- Addressing issues without a fear of retaliation.
- A particular student's behavior. (One teacher and I'm sure more has had parents ask what they did to make the kid act that way. Ha, hate to be the one to break your delusions, but you're kid's probably a jerk because of homelife not school.)
- Not letting a student use the restroom immediately. – (There are some kids who have an accommodation that

they can use it for medical reasons, but 90% of the kids are using the excuse to take a walk and play on their phones.)

Note: I stopped checking around comment 400, this isn't checking the sub responses, which are mostly people just agreeing or telling their personal stories that reinforces the point. They just started repeating.

Conclusion:

Teaching is an awesome profession, but there's a lot messed up about how it's perceived by the wider world. Hopefully, communication can improve some of this. If you're ever curious, just watch some of the social media reels put out by teachers. They're not always accurate, but they are usually entertaining.

Chapter 59:
Episode 179 – General Opinion:
Lockdown Part 1 – What Happened.

Introduction:

Lockdown is not my favorite word, but it's become a part of the drill culture of modern American schools.

This is also not my favorite week.

What happened:

Tuesday started like any other. It was one of my easy days. I happened to be testing my students. It should have been the last two classes to see the test because the other two had already taken it on Monday.

This is my early/light day. I see a class, have a study hall duty, then a period off. The next block is lunch. First half, I have a hall duty right outside the cafeteria. It's usually a good time to eat my lunch or relax a bit before my lab and class.

About 7-8 minutes before the lab should switch over, ending my duty, I see a pretty blue light at the end of the time.

I remember thinking: *That's a pretty blue light. Oh crap.*

The PA system didn't say anything immediately, which is weird. So, like most people, I stood there a few seconds and stared at the dumb thing. Then, I either faintly heard the system trying to tell us it was a lockdown or finally got the brain in working order.

Anyway, I went into the lunchroom. There were also blue lights inside the cafeteria. Some people were slowly meandering toward the kitchen and the teacher's cafeteria, which is located next to the kitchen.

I hurried them along. Told a few lingering groups to head into the teacher's cafeteria. Went into sheepherding mode and helped other teachers get the lot of them into the back room.

Went to check on one of the side doors to the lunchroom. An admin came in at the same time. I asked him if the door was locked, and he confirmed it was. (I probably should have double checked myself.)

Waited for the last few near me to get in the door then went in and locked it with my key. Had to open it to check the lock thing worked from my side. I moved further into the room.

At first, there was a bit of room to move around and breathe, but then, they started to let people in from the kitchen.

It got tighter. I encouraged a few groups to move to open space because they were clumping. Finally, I figured they can do what they want and took up a post near the door I'd locked where another teacher stood. The admin who I'd spoken to about the other door being locked came in the side entrance and stood near that.

There was a general buzz of excited, nervous chatter. I didn't think that was wise but hoped the admin would say something. Dude makes 2x what I do easily. It's kinda his job to keep order.

Once everybody was reasonably settled, we waited.

At one point, more kids came in from the kitchen. The noise level rose.

A woman was shouting from the kitchen. I couldn't hear words, but I gathered she was trying to get the kids to shut up.

The admin eventually raised his voice and shouted the kids down to some level of quiet. I heard him mutter something about he didn't know why she wanted them to be quiet, but they should do it anyway.

Uh, sir, what do you mean, you don't know why we're supposed to be quiet during a lockdown event?

Most kids had their phones. One smart kid had grabbed his lunch and was chowing down on the sandwich.

The teacher's cafeteria was standing room only in many parts, but the section near me had a bit of space.

Eventually, we started telling kids they should sit down if they can because we don't know how long it would last. Some listened. Some didn't. I didn't worry about those who didn't.

I did tell the kids standing near me to take their backpacks off. That was mostly because the kid kept moving, bringing his backpack right near my face.

And we waited some more.

After an eternity (about an hour and 10 minutes), a cop came in, got everyone's attention, and asked if someone needed medical help. He explained that it would be a few more minutes, but they still needed to clear the building.

We waited some more.

Finally, another cop came in and told us we could move to the lunchroom proper.

I didn't realize at the time that it was still a shelter in place, but I got the idea we weren't supposed to leave the lunchroom.

A kid asked me if he could leave. Had to tell him no. (I believe a parent was coming to pick him up.)

Lines formed and the kids got to get food. Many hadn't had a chance because it was early enough in the lunchtime that they never made it through the line.

Another admin asked me to stand by the lunch line and keep order. Wasn't exactly sure what to do, but the kids were good about forming a line with minimal cutting. I stood by the exit door to make sure people were leaving and not sneaking in through that way.

Once the line diminished, I left my post and wandered down to the other end of the cafeteria to talk to a friend who had lunch duty. (She got stuck in the kitchen during the wait.)

At last, around 12:30 we got an announcement from the principal that the high school would have an early dismissal and all after school activities were canceled.

Next up:
Stories (and reflections) from the Great Lockdown.

Chapter 60:
Episode 180 – General Opinion:
Lockdown Part 2 - Reflections

Introduction:

During the Great Lockdown of 2024 (as one colleague jokingly put it), I was stuck on the longest lunch duty of my entire life.

But in all fairness, I did not have it the worst.

What follows is only a very tiny fraction of the stories I'm sure exist about the event.

I'll also throw in some reflections.

Disclaimer: As far as I know these stories are correct, but they aren't all mine. I heard from someone who heard from someone else in most cases.

The Good:

- The kids with me and at least one other teacher and one admin were generally good. It was a very long time to be standing there not knowing much. Some chattered, but most were good about following the instruction to keep quiet.

- (If it had been a lockdown with an active shooter, the person would have to be stone cold deaf not to have heard them, but to be fair, if they had any sense of the school day, they'd know it was lunch time. There's only so many places that will fit a few hundred students.)
- Nobody with me had a nervous breakdown, though I think a few kids were getting anxious.

The Crazy:
- As the lockdown was being called, I was on the phone with my doctor's office getting some test results.
- I had to tell this woman, "I've got to call you back. We're in the middle of a lockdown. Just message me the details. I'll get to it when I can."

The Dumb:
- One of the teachers tried to hide to see how well they would search the building.
- Me: Are you out of your mind? These people don't know what's happening. They're probably hopped up on adrenaline and itching to do something. You're lucky nobody shot you. (The principal had to vouch for the teacher with the cop who found him.)

The Scary Awards:
- One of the math teachers was using the restroom at the time the lockdown was called. He spent the entire time there. When it finally let up, a cop came in and searched the bathroom. Had a gun in this guy's face for a hot second.
- A substitute teacher was in the room with some of the special ed kids. The subs don't have keys to the rooms. So,

this poor lady was stuck for an hour and a half with the half-dozen kids who clock the highest anxiety levels with a door that doesn't lock. They moved a couch in front of the door.

The Expected:

- The kids knew way more than the staff during the event.
- During the wait, I mentioned to the teacher with me that the best-case scenario is that it's a system malfunction. Told a few curious kids that too by way of explaining why we still had to wait awhile longer.
- Communication to teachers was abysmal. Most of us stayed in some sort of loop based on personal chats with colleagues in our department. (There probably should be a better system than our automated one because clearly, that doesn't always work. Even if we gotta go old school and do a department group text or something.)
- The principal and the superintendent both sent emails around.
- Principal's email thanked everybody for their professionalism. Told us the company was here and replacing some stuff. "Let's hope that will solve the issue." He also said he'd be in one of the theaters tomorrow if we had questions.
- The superintendent's actually sent two emails. Her first said that the chief of police would leave an officer outside the high school. Classes would resume. We're safe. The lockdown will lift soon. We're looking into the cause of the malfunction.
- Her second email was sent to everybody (not just high school staff). It said today was stressful. Explained that the high school went into a lockdown around 11. It was a malfunction, is being fixed, and school's on at normal time tomorrow. There was an early dismissal because they

wanted to avoid further panic in case it went off again. She also mentioned that she is required to lockdown wherever she's at in the building (that's the protocol). Letter closed with a some good came of it missive and a general apology for the stress.

- Police from 3 departments helped. (The news article cited more.)
- They brought out the county SWAT team.
- The police chief said students and staff followed appropriate protocols and figuratively patted our heads for the professionalism and cooperation. The school is safe and secure.

The Unexpected:
- I heard kids in the kitchens tried to climb on counters (got yelled at by the staff there).
- Also heard (from kids) that people were stealing food and Gatorade.
- Some kids didn't get lunch that day because the lockdown was called before the end of the first lab period. Everybody in lab was stuck in a classroom, and everybody who went to see a teacher for a makeup test or extra help was stuck away from the lunchroom.

The Unspoken:
- Some people did more than others.
- After the kids got back to the lunchroom, there were some Chapters of cheering, table banging, and climbing over tables. (Not very "professional" if you ask me. Not one admin stepped up to address them about the behavior.)
- The word professionalism came up a lot. I get that you don't want to admit it but for a while there nobody knew what the heck was happening. (I said the county should thank us for the very nice joint drill.) Things ran smoothly

enough, but it also brought to light the terrible communication skills from school leadership.

Conclusion:

It was the best-case scenario. I definitely could do with less excitement. I'm highly doubtful any meaningful change will happen now that it's over.

The End ... for now.

Thank You for Reading:

Dear Reader,

This book would never have happened without the Vella program.

Special thanks to everybody who agreed to do interviews.

Schools have all kinds of stakeholders. Each person has a vested interest in seeing students succeed. It's been interesting to hear from some of the many perspectives out there.

If you'd like to keep up with my work, email **devyaschildren@gmail.com** and/or sign up for my newsletter on my website. (**juliecgilbert.com**)

Sincerely,

Ann Y. Mouse
(Julie C. Gilbert)

Love Science Fiction or Mystery?

Choose your adventure!

Visit: **http://www.juliecgilbert.com/**

For details on getting free books

www.ingramcontent.com/pod-product-compliance
Lightning Source LLC
LaVergne TN
LVHW051224080426
835513LV00016B/1391